Kamron, Mom, Don, Shannon, Pam… November, 1972

Gun To The Head
MARKETING

KAMRON KARINGTON

Published by Raptor Press
Kamron Karington
Visit my website at www.karingtongroup.com
Printed in the United States of America
First Printing: February 2010

ISBN 978-1-4276-4555-5

Preface .... *i*

Prelude 1
   Saturday Morning. August 16, 1974 1
   The Rolling Stones 10
   Ghost from Summer's Past 14

Gun to the Head Marketing 16
   Dark, Illuminating Thoughts 16
   123% Sales Increase in 30 Days 18
   Marketing Intervention 20

Force Multiplier 27
   Controlling Fire 28
   Money Maze 30
   Become Your Customer 33
   Movie Stars & Money 36
   Mind Control 37
   Phineas Gage 42
   Triple Threat 43
   The 10% Solution 44

Attract More Customers 46
   Message Control 47
   Persuasion Equation 50
   Headless Body in Topless Bar 53
   Visual Gulps 57
   Balance of Power 67
   Thought Control 68
   Buying Triggers 74
   Anchors 82
   Subliminal Control 83
   Passion Control 90
   Bullets 92

Proof 96

Morphine Marketing 105

Offer 110

Connect the Dots 114

Open Loop 115

What to Sell 117

Profit Control 123

Competitor Control 126

Take Away 130

Call to Action 132

Trojan Horse 133

The Two-Step 139

Cash Control 141

Growth Control 142

Mr. Olympia 145

Allow Customers to Spend More Money 148

Selling Sentences 149

You Don't Say? 150

Enjoy More Customer Visits 158

The Peter Principle 160

Mass Advertising is Dead 162

World of Mouth 165

Rage Control 167

Desperation Versus Appreciation 168

Customer Control 170

Combination to the Safe 174

Death Spiral 178

Epilogue 181

Afterword 183

Preface

On November 18, 1518, Hernando Cortéz and a small force set sail from Santiago, Spain. Three and a half grueling months later, they landed on the shores of the Yucatan Peninsula off modern day Mexico. Cortéz unloaded his men and supplies, and then promptly – *set his 11 ships on fire…*

There would be no turning back. His life now depended on his every decision.

One year to the date since he left Spain, Cortéz entered the Aztec capital and imprisoned Montezuma. With a force of fewer than 600 men, 20 horses, and 10 canons, Hernando Cortéz invaded and conquered the Aztec empire populated by more than 5 million people. Never before had such a small force conquered and seized such vast wealth. Without adequate forces, outnumbered 8000 to 1, and against all odds – Cortéz conquered an entire nation.

About this same time, and not very far away at all, Ferdinand Magellan crossed the equator on a daring and terrifying voyage to claim a westward route to the Spice Islands. Victory was fleeting though as he became obsessed, and sidetracked with converting Philippine natives to Christianity. Invincibility and arrogance seized his mind, and in the end, his crossbows and cannons proved useless and he was butchered on Mactan Island by an agitated pack of natives wielding makeshift weapons. Magellan was bold, confident, self-assured… and dead.

Cortéz too, was a study in confidence, but also a master of motivation. Mountains of rumored gold were the single obsessive driving force. And while filling their pockets with gold must have been a pleasant thought to his men... witnessing their only means of escape blazing offshore must have erased any thoughts of failure. Madness? Maybe. Maybe not.

The distinction between brilliant action and reckless insanity can only be measured by the razor-thin line of victory. And victory was his.

Today in business we see the very same forces at work. Glory in the form of money, freedom and ego, drive some to step away from cozy nine to five jobs and risk it all. Most are quickly sucked into the deep dark, unforgiving trenches of failure. Some though... very few indeed, rise to unimaginable heights and spectacular success.

What little things do *they* do differently? What decisions dramatically alter the trajectory of *their* lives and put *them* in the winners circle? What questions do *they* ask... and what answers do *they* receive?

Our journey begins in Hell.

Prelude

Saturday Morning. August 16, 1974

Kamron… wake up… get up… we're going for a ride. The voice was familiar… then I noticed the revolver. A squat 38 snub-nose. I'd fired that gun many times myself. It was waving back and forth… not threatening… more like a person would wave a finger to motion you to action.

The right hand of my step-father, Donald Eugene Stewart, held the gun… his left hand had a firm grip on my mother.

Using the gun as an extension of his hand Don kept jabbing it at my mother to menace and gain compliance…

Today… we were "going for a ride." This was unusual… previously the violence had always happened right here in the house. There was still a bullet hole in the floor of the master bedroom… and the sewing machine had never looked the same since it had been hurled down the basement stairs.

I put on my pants. No shirt, no shoes… just pants.

After rounding up my mother, my younger sister Shannon, and me, we piled into my mom's white 65 Mustang and began a short drive down 45th South. Don directed the scene from the passenger seat… my mother at the wheel. As we neared a small office building near our house, Don barked out: "Pull in here!" My mom, thinking he meant the

7-Eleven right next door… flew right past the office building, and into the crowded parking lot.

Don jabbed the gun at her side screaming: "Get out of here… get out of here – now!"

The Mustang swerved in a screeching gravel-spewing circle through the 7-Eleven parking lot… there was quite a buzz of people and activity at the entry of the store. Necks craned and bodies tensed when our Mustang came barreling through the lot.

I sat, sequestered in the passenger-side backseat… taking it all in as though watching a tornado… suddenly, a pair of eyes in this blur locked onto mine as though drawn by powerful gravity.

They were familiar. But unexpected. My older sister Pam was standing outside the store's entry.

I was puzzled. Why wasn't she still in bed? Then I became more puzzled… why wasn't *she* with *us*? In an instant, I understood. She'd heard the commotion upstairs and fled to call the police… an auto-pilot response instilled by Don's habit of ripping the phone out of the wall prior to a rampage.

Her eyes carried simultaneous but conflicting emotions. Emotions that can't even exist side-by-side. Emotions that can't emulsify – even for a short time like oil and vinegar.

Not the helpless look one might feel as a bystander to an unfolding tragedy… but something entirely different.

A combined look of doom, and dread and terror… coupled with an oddly reassuring comfort… a haunting gaze that I'd never seen before, and I've never seen since…

Funny, how adrenaline can sharpen your senses and turn time into still-frames that move one at a time… each one being analyzed for critical clues that may hold a secret to survival.

From that fraction of a second, frozen like a photograph in my mind… I pondered mortality. The doom, the dread, the terror in *her* eyes… transferred to me.

Today *would* be different from all the rest. The Don I knew was *not* in the car. "This Don" was dictating orders as though detached from his own body. This Don was wearing a crazed, never-before-seen expression. This Don seemed to have a step-by-step plan. This Don was waaaay out of character.

We were now in the office parking lot where Don had intended us to go in the first place. Odd… we were now switching to a green Ford Pinto that he'd rented and concealed prior to slipping into the house through an open window. Further indication that things were just getting started. Why a rental car? Probably so the cops can't spot us in the Mustang…

Then it hit me…

My sister's expression… an expression that no actor could ever replicate – the odd reassuring nature of it… the comforting under-tone… had whispered: "Don't worry Kam… the cops are coming… you'll be okay." We always ran to the 7-Eleven to call the cops. We accelerated onto the 215 northbound freeway from the brand new onramp that had just been completed. The speed limit was 55… the speedometer neared 70.

7 Minutes After Waking Up…

"Slow down… slow the car down!"

Frightened out of her mind, with a lunatic pressing a pistol into her side, in a car she'd never driven before… my mom tapped the brake.

And then in a blinding instant… one of those instances that cannot ever be recalled… an instant that can never be taken back or lived over… an instant frozen in time… thunder exploded, Don's hand snapped back, my mother slumped over the wheel… a bluish-grey haze of freshly burned gun powder filled the car.

My eyes, ears and nostrils recorded these individual occurrences... as a single event. One can never be isolated in time from the others.

The bullet had already seared completely through my mother of course, before the sound, site – and what it meant collided in my mind. Christ! She's been shot!

Deceleration...

"Drive!"

"I can't..."

"Drive the car!"

"Don, you've shot me..."

"You're not shot."

"Kamron, I love you... tell your sisters I love them... I love you... tell your sisters I love them..."

"Don – we need to get her to a hospital..."

"Don!? We've got to get her to a hospital!"

Time was now being measured in light-years...

Disbelief swims through Don's eyes... but he can't blink away the carnage. And so now, adrift on a highway to hell, the driverless Pinto has become a wayward missile... seeking a target.

Donald Eugene Stewart never utters another word.

But mothers possess a strength that only mothers know... a strength born of birth itself.

Through the millennia, mothers have sacrificed their own shelter, their own food, their own lives... for their children. Nature has inspired them to great achievement when danger visits.

Today though, my mother would not fight off menacing attackers, she would not charge into a blazing inferno, she would not even illuminate a nightlight to ward off the monsters that lay just beneath my young sister's cradle.

No… today, my mother would perform none of those fearless deeds. Today, she would simply lift her frail, shaking, bloody hands to the wheel… and mount a titanic struggle through hot, engulfing and uncontainable pain… to deliver her children gently to the safety of the emergency lane…

Her mission complete, her voice softer now… "Kamron I love you… tell your sisters I love them…"

Those words, at *that* moment have proven to be the most precious gift I've ever received from my mother. But now… the second bomb was ticking…

As though controlled by a master out to erase his mistake…. or a robot pre-programmed to attach a fender on a factory's assembly line, Don went about his work…

He engages the cylinder release and ejects the contents into his hand. He's visibly puzzled when he – does in fact – notice an empty "still smoking" spent cartridge. This particular Smith and Wesson 38 snub… had an unbelievably treacherous "hair trigger." And the gun had in truth… accidentally gone off when my mom tapped the brake pedal.

Fired point-blank – in a near perfect horizontal trajectory, the bullet, traveling at 1,000 feet per second sprouts claws and seeks a destructive path.

Hemorrhaging begins immediately. Burgundy blood squirts and seeps from two wounds with each heartbeat.

The lead from this vacant shell – after a tour of my mother's digestive system, including the blood-rich liver, pancreas, gall bladder, and small intestine… rested now, in the driver's side door panel. Don quickly and methodically reloads the weapon, almost as though trying to set a new world's speed-loading record.

"Don – we've got to get her to a hospital…"

And then, without the slightest reservation or hesitation, he lifts the gun to his right temple, cocks it – and squeezes the trigger… "click."

He cocks and squeezes again… this time he hits pay-dirt, and executes the final, willful action of his life.

Another ear-splitting explosion is instantly replaced with deafening silence. A silence you would find on the surface of the moon. Tunnel vision has erased the world outside.

And like a vigorously shaken, freshly uncorked bottle of Champagne on New Year's Eve… the left half of Don's head, the home of logic, and reason, and contemplation explodes in a macabre spray. As is common with loud noises and unexpected sights, I jerk and twitch and blink involuntarily. Then the bleeding begins.

In the absence of muscle control, Don's head rolls grotesquely to the left. The torrent is unbelievable. A violent flow… that to this day reminds me of a fire hose unleashing a pumping blood-bath. Not at all like those old movies where you'd see a little red drip when someone takes a bullet to the head. No. This was more like something from the opening scenes of "Saving Private Ryan."

More smoke. More blood. More reason to get the fuck out of this death trap and find… no… *demand* help. I'll run across the freeway to the grocery store… no… that'll take decades. I'll, I'll…

Then I realize my predicament…

I am trapped in the backseat of a two-door Ford Pinto. My feet are warm. Why did I think about that? But I did?

There's little chance I can escape this death compartment from the passenger side… Don is literally – dead weight now.

"Mom! Open the door… open the door…"

Silence.

Slow motion ends… time accelerates…

Don's corpse is a formidable barrier… I have no choice. My right hand must find the seat latch, my left hand will clutch at Don's hair… the seat will go forward, I'll yank the door handle – and let gravity guide Don to the waiting cement. Where's the latch? Where's the fuck-ing latch!?

Then, barely audible at first… I heard the driver's side door latch disengage… my mom was still alive and had marshaled enough strength to free me from this blood-soaked nightmare.

I exploded between the seat and the door-jamb like a wild animal escaping a cage… I still remember my bare feet. The warmth… the pavement. I circle around the front of the car…

Years earlier, during one of Don's first episodes – I ran to our neighbor's house and as I approached I made a snap decision… instead of knocking and waiting for an answer… I'd just try the handle. The door *was* unlocked and I burst in to the front room of a very stunned Sam and Bernice Soter screaming "Don's gotta gun!"

Today required a similar approach. Something a little more aggressive than waving my hands at traffic from the emergency lane in the hopes that someone would eventually pull over.

To be sure, what I did next was not bravery… my actions were propelled by savage instincts and stone-cold shock. The same chemicals anyone would be swimming in when confronted by a bloody "multiple" shooting – seven minutes after getting out of bed.

I quickly figure – the fastest way to get help for my mother is to insist that someone stop. Someone can drive to the store and call an ambulance – much faster than I can run to the store. Then I change my mind… *everyone's* going to stop.

My eyes fix on the freeway behind the Pinto. There's a brief opening in the traffic. Oh yeah… there're cars coming… but right now – this very instant – I can stop them all.

Fueled by shock, panic and adrenaline – I rapidly march out… not "in front" of… but at a 45 degree angle – towards and "into" oncoming traffic… my arms spread out as wide as they'll go. Ten feet wide. Twenty feet wide. I commanded my arms to spread so far that nothing could pass… nothing… nothing. Not a molecule.

In just seconds, with the stink and squeal of rubber on pavement… the freeway became a parking lot.

I'm spinning in circles screaming at anybody, somebody, every-body… "Call an ambulance… call an ambulance!"

At the same time one of the very first drivers who found themselves on a collision course with a 15-year-old-kid, in the middle of a freeway, on a warm August morning… pulled over just in front of the Pinto. He was driving a van.

The good Samaritan had no possible idea of the carnage and horror he was about to stumble into. Amazingly, as I screamed about my mother being shot… he raced faster to the car as though a bullet-proof force-field would protect him from the shooter.

As he helped my mother to his van I ran back to get Shannon. That's when I heard the first siren in the distance.

My sister had come through… the cops were on their way… and thanks to Pam… they were headed in the right direction.

I pulled Shannon from the clutches of Hell… and at the same time, I noticed something unexpected. Don was still alive.

What seemed like just minutes after escaping the bloodbath… the freeway looked like a Sheriff's Convention… my sister Pam arrived… ambulances arrived… and the news media were already whipping out notepads and setting up cameras…

And just like that… the first 19 minutes of my day – were gone.

But even as my mother's ambulance pulled onto the freeway, racing to Saint Mark's Hospital… darkness was beginning to nibble at the outer regions of her vision. A tunnel was forming. Darkness invited her to sleep. And so she did.

Salt lake County Sheriff, Dick Fisher, invited me into his patrol car for a ride to the hospital.

During the short journey, the radio crackled… "What's your ETA?" "Inbound… ETA three minutes." "What are we looking at?" "Most likely two DOAs."

Dick quickly snatched the microphone from its mounting post on the cruiser's dashboard… "Uhm… the victim's son is in my car… I'm switching off… over."

"Clear!"

Electric paddles exploded. My mother's lifeless body jerked six inches off the Emergency room gurney. Nothing. Clear… but then a faint heartbeat flickered… a tether to this world was reestablished.

After 1,000 volts of heart-starting electricity, 33 pints of life sustaining blood, and 5 hours of careful painstaking suturing… my mother was wheeled into ICU clinging to life. Don, I was informed… rested quietly in a body bag in the hospital's cooler.

Hours later, sitting in the Intensive Care waiting room, wearing my jeans and a borrowed hospital smock… my eyes began to focus. My feet were purple-black… as though I were wearing shoes of dried blood. That explained the warmth.

I managed to get one foot at a time into a bathroom sink… and rinsed away the day's blood, brains and gore. As the hypnotic effect of lumpy pink fluid circling down the drain slowly faded… I caught a glance at myself in the mirror. I realized… I would also need to wash my face.

That's my last memory from that day.

Twenty years later I woke up from a very disturbed sleep… on top of a walk-in cooler, in a run-down pizzeria… with a most puzzling question that seemed eerily connected to the past…

Here's where it gets weird…

The Rolling Stones

November, 1994... the big news was announced. The Rolling Stones are coming to Salt Lake City, Utah. I simply must have tickets... good ones too.

A few days after the tickets sold out, I thumbed through the Salt Lake Tribune classified section till I found the "Tickets for sale" heading. I circled a few numbers... grabbed the phone and dialed...

The odds of being struck by a meteorite have to be better than the odds of what happened in the next 45 seconds. But then again... odd things happen every day... we just often – don't tie tectonic shifts in the direction of our lives to happenstance.

The conversation:

"Hello..."

"Hey... calling about your Rolling Stone's tickets... do you still have them?"

"Yes I do..."

"Great... can you tell me the section, row and seat numbers please?"

(This I don't remember... but they were not seats that I was interested in)...

"Hmmmm? You know... I'm looking for something a bit closer to the stage... I'm going to pass on these... thank you"

I was about to hang up... when he said: "You wouldn't want to buy my Pizzeria would you?"

"Uh... no... (pause) where is it?"

...Three days later I became the proud owner of a neglected run-down, nearly bankrupt pizzeria with only one single, solitary, redeeming quality. The product was "over the top..." and I was certain of success.

The business was completely staffed with order-takers, cooks and a manager. Accounts were in place. Equipment was humming along. If ever a turn-key business was ripe for the picking... this was it. What kind of idiot could possibly screw this up?

The keys were handed over in the evening… the crew would be notified of the ownership change… and the next day I'd set about turning this ugly duckling into a beautiful swan.

By 11:15 the next morning, fully half of the crew had walked off the job. Those that remained were mostly dope-smoking idiots. The hook wouldn't stay attached to the dough mixer (now I knew what that piece of coat-hanger wire I'd tossed in the trash was used for). The refrigeration had issues which escalated into the entire day's batch of dough exploding to ten times its normal size… engulfing a third of the walk-in. It was, in a way – like waking up from a nap and finding yourself freezing, wet and alone, in a violent storm in the middle of the Atlantic Ocean… 1,000 miles from shore.

My "auto-pilot" business… was already off the hinges… and we weren't even open for lunch yet. Great.

Of course, things proceeded downhill from there…

The next few weeks brought uncertainty in my decision. Doubt seeped in. Second guessing began. Had I just committed the biggest blunder of my life?

Nancy and I were thrust into open-to-close shifts… we hardly saw our daughter anymore… home was just a place to shower and sleep… Make no mistake… what "owned" what was very clear. I was no business owner. I was a slave. My new business owned me, lock, stock and barrel.

How did I miscalculate so badly? My days as a cook at J.B.'s Big-Boy seemed so carefree. I loved going to work. I enjoyed the friendship… it was fun.

But that was a lifetime ago…

Ninth Grade... Three and a half months after Don splattered the contents of his skull in that green Pinto, my drug and alcohol use had escalated a bit. This particular early afternoon found me in Mrs. Wilson's English class flying high on two hits of LSD.

Mrs. Wilson had obviously spotted my detachment because she made an unusual request of me. "Kamron, will you please read the next paragraph?"

Not knowing what paragraph she referred to, or even what page we were on – was the least of my problems.

As I studied the book... each letter, on each page appeared to be punched out as though I was holding a stencil... as though – if you went outdoors and held the page up, blue sky would come through each letter.

I was indoors of course, and in the absence of black ink – or blue sky... a rainbow of brilliant, intense psychedelic colors swirled behind each letter replacing the black ink that should have been present.

I closed the book after a moment, looked up at Mrs. Wilson and said: "I can't read."

And with that, my eyes began searching for the door... upon locating it, I pondered the epic journey... then began moving towards it as though wearing cement boots. The door seemed to keep receding as though it were taking a step back for every step I took forward. Eventually I twisted the handle and freed myself from English class.

Eighth grade became the last completed year of school for me. I never returned. A few weeks later I was having the time of my life grilling burgers at J.B.'s Big-Boy.

And so the decision was made. While J.B.'s Big-Boy had been a scene out of "Happy days" – this was pure unadulterated Hell. Within 30 days of having the keys dropped into my hand, I arrived at the conclusion that I had, in fact – made a horrible mistake. Spruce the place up a bit... and dump it. Dump it fast.

So, a few nights later after closing… a tattooed, nearly toothless, red-haired, hot-tempered ex-con demolished the front counter with a sledgehammer. The "sprucing up had begun." His name was "Richard" And he could single-handedly build a mansion from scrap found on the side of the road. He had an amazing talent for carpentry… and in between wild, booze-fueled binges… he built beautiful things.

He figured the tear-down and rebuild would take till about 2 am. And even though my eyes already looked like roadmaps – knowing Richard, I thought it wise to supervise the project and stay close by.

Already beat from long days and sleepless nights, I was struggling to stay focused when Richard started… but by 3:30 am, an hour and a half behind schedule… I was toast. Driving home to a warm comfortable bed was no longer an option.

I told Richard: "Listen dude… I'm going to crawl up on the walk-in cooler in back and grab some shut-eye… just lock the door and close it behind you when you're finished."

We stored unfolded pizza boxes on top of the walk-in. Seemed like a cardboard bed was better than the floor.

So I crawled up, squeezed in, spread out some boxes, lowered my head and closed my eyes. Exhaustion went to work, pulling me towards sleep. But disappointment temporarily halted the journey.

At the age of 4, when my mom was late picking me up from nursery school… I began the voyage home by myself, on foot – on the side of a busy highway. I nearly made it too, but a concerned neighbor spotted me and insisted that she give me a ride the remaining half mile. I was disappointed. I knew my mom would be so proud of me walking home by myself. In reality she was at the school in near hysteria hunting for any signs of my whereabouts.

I'd managed to pull out an amazing win after being nearly check-mated during a 4th-grade chess tournament. My opponent had me on the run for most of the game. I felt sure I'd be humiliated in front of the swelling crowd that had gathered to witness my certain defeat. My win stunned the chess teacher and everyone watching.

I'd hitch-hiked from Salt Lake to San Diego when I was 14. I had earned a pilot's license and owned an airplane when I was 23. I'd opened four nightclubs by the time I was 30... and produced a hit record with 4 top-10 singles on the Billboard Dance Chart... one even cracked the Billboard Top-40 chart... I was 31 then.

So why then, was I being so easily defeated by this rinky-dink pizzeria? What was so tough about this? All it really needed were more sales, which would lead to profits, which would lead to hiring good people which would lead to the freedom that most people go into business for in the first place. What *would* it take to quickly and dramatically raise sales?

Ghost from Summer's Past

Richard's hammer pounded. Bang... bang... bang. Strange voices echo from far   away... Gremlins appear from dark shadows... a disturbing visitor grips my mother's arm and says: "Kamron, wake up... get up, we're going for a ride." And like so many times before, Don's ghost returned. And behind closed eyelids, a kaleidoscopic dream of a long ago morning, began again.

Kamron... wake up...

Nancy, concerned that I'd not made it home, came to the shop first thing in the morning and discovered me passed out on the walk-in. She was now headed to the 7-Eleven to get me some much-needed coffee.

The mental fog was clearing but reality hesitated... I wandered into the dining area to see Richard's completed work. I was perplexed by how he'd applied the Formica. The edges that go around the side should be tucked under the top piece to prevent the sides from catching and chipping.

Richard had done the opposite. I knew it would be trouble. But that would be the next owner's problem...

Alone, in my pizzeria – waiting for a cup of coffee, a few days before Christmas... surrounded by chairs, tables, dreams and disappointment... sadness seemed my only possession.

Then oddly enough, while absentmindedly gazing out the window... looking at nothing in particular... a spark ignited... my eyes flicked back and forth... my lips tightened. I was on to something.

Slowly, as though in a trance, I made my way to Richard's brand new counter to locate a pen and scrap of paper... oddly the Formica really bothered me now – and I vaguely knew why... a minute ago – it was someone else's problem... now it was mine.

But first... puzzling, lurking in the back of my mind, almost beyond my ability to recognize it... a question was struggling to take shape. It would break through any second. And I always write down what seems important at the time.

And so, a restless night on top of a walk-in cooler, a troubled search for an exit from a disaster, and the tip of a 10 cent Bic ballpoint pen produced the following:

"If someone held a gun to my head and told me I needed to get one brand new customer to buy a pizza at full price within 24 hours or they would pull the trigger... what would I do?"

The answer to that question changed the course of my life.

Gun to the Head Marketing

A dark question illuminates an amazing journey…

Dark, Illuminating Thoughts

Just think of how empowering that mindset is. You'd do just about anything to avoid the most serious consequences of failure. You'll dig deeper, reach further and stretch wider than you ever imagined… if only – your life depended on it.

But I'm not talking about some casual thought of some vague gun in the hands of some indistinct boogeyman…

You MUST internalize the "feeling" to gain the power of its motivation.

Imagine… feeling the cold steel circle of a gun barrel pressing at your temple. Hearing the metallic "click" as the hammer is set into place… the primer at the base of the brass shell casing anxiously awaiting the arrival of an oh so eager firing pin to release it's spark… which in turn ignites a death-dealing detonation that forces the business-end of the bullet to shatter your skull with the explosive force of dynamite… the lead, now horribly disfigured from the initial impact – sprouts wings… jagged wings and jagged edges and jagged claws. Not slicing cleanly and precisely as a surgeon's sharp blade might… but tearing and ripping and hacking. Your thoughts, your memories, your loved ones dissolve as the lead carves its gruesome path. After destroying a lifetime of life… it breaks free in a gaping, bloody spraying geyser of gore. Your heart explodes like a jackhammer… faster and faster in a futile attempt to restore your quickly failing blood pressure. A temporary burst of consciousness flickers as more and more blood races to replace the pumping torrent. For a few terrifying moments you beg for death… and finally, after gasping and gurgling for what seems like a time without end… the cold, deep vacuum of eternity pulls you into its inescapable grasp.

Okay… now snap out of it! It's not a pretty picture. Believe me – *I know*.

But *that* frame of mind – to avoid *those* consequences… will open a treasure trove of resources that cannot be unlocked or explored by the simple question: "How can I make more money." No.

"What would I do if my life *depended* on making more money?"

That's a different question altogether.

Just like a snorkeler off Maui would claw and pull and rip at the ocean with super-human strength upon hearing someone scream "Shark!!!" versus just simply returning to the boat when someone screams "cold beer!"

…So too, will the "right" question immediately unlock vast where-withal, powerful insights and unwavering self-assurance that lays buried just beneath the surface of day-to-day complacency.

Within moments of jotting down that oh-so perplexing question my "ah-ha" moment arrived, and crystallized into a clear plan of action.

123% Sales Increase in 30 Days

With the clock ticking, I formulated my survival plan. Over the next 30 days, my sales increased 123%. Three years later, we were doing over a million and a half dollars a year with a peak increase of 1,066% from the day I bought the place. We were now doing in seven days, what used to take two and a half months. We used a machine to count the money.

And to be sure, this is not a story about "Kamron" the marketing genius, but more the story of a very lucky man standing on the shoulders *of* geniuses. I've simply followed brilliant visionaries who've illuminated vast expanses of darkness, and were gracious enough to leave the lights on, share their discoveries and pass their knowledge down through time. I've enjoyed tremendous success as a result.

I've also been fortunate in being able to share my discoveries with thousands of business owners from coast to coast and around the world. One of them is a billion dollar company. Many are in the $2 to $20 million range. However, most are small but very fierce independent business owners.

It's immensely gratifying to hear heart-warming stories from people whose lives have been permanently enriched by their newfound marketing skills.

This ninth-grade drop out is very humbled and grateful.

Can You Sell Apples… and Oranges Too?

I've been a lifelong student of marketing. I've rubbed shoulders with some of the biggest names in the biz. Jay Abraham, John Carlton, Gary Bencivenga, Brian Keith Voiles, and Gary Halbert… to name a handful.

And not once, have I ever studied "Pizza Marketing." Quite the contrary. I intensely studied the geniuses who sold Bissell carpet sweepers, golf clubs, books, shoe polish, Rolls Royces, investment newsletters, Icy-Hot… even lard. Not one single shred of what I learned to build my sales by over 1,000 percent was the result of studying "pizza marketing."

And as the late, great Gary Halbert once said: "I could spend three days teaching 100 people everything I know about selling more apples than anyone else on earth. And there would always be some idiot who would say 'Yeah, but I sell oranges… how does this help me?'" Sadly, some people just suffer from aggressive stupidity. Fact is… restaurant and pizza marketing is fiercely competitive. Learning what works in that arena is like acquiring a tenth-degree Black Belt. Probably more skill than you'll ever fully need. But it's sure nice to have, when you find yourself navigating a dark alley.

And guess what? Even though I'm famous for helping pizzeria and restaurant owners… I've also been instrumental in helping other businesses grow sales. Everything from a company that sells tools to the airline industry, to a major financial institution.

Today, my company, Repeat Returns – handles day-to-day marketing for grocery stores, bowling alleys, pet stores, beauty shops, dry-cleaners, and yes… even restaurants.

So, if you can learn to sell apples, it shouldn't be too big a leap to selling fruit… to selling vegetables… to selling Plasma TVs.

Marketing Intervention

Back in the late 1800s, early 1900s, advertising was deeply mired in the dark ages. Ad agencies believed that good advertising was – *"Keeping One's Name Before the Public."* Commonly known as "image advertising."

The lights came on bright, when at six o'clock on a May evening in 1904, a very self-confident Canadian by the name of John E. Kennedy waltzed into Chicago's Lord & Thomas Ad Agency. He asked that a note be dispatched to Mr. Thomas, President of the agency. It read:

"DEAR MR. THOMAS, I AM DOWNSTAIRS. I KNOW WHAT ADVERTISING IS. I KNOW YOU DON'T KNOW. IT WILL MEAN MUCH TO ME TO HAVE YOU KNOW WHAT IT IS AND IT WILL MEAN MUCH TO YOU. IF YOU WISH TO KNOW WHAT ADVERTISING IS, TELL THIS MESSENGER THAT I SHOULD COME UP."

JOHN E. KENNEDY.

The word "yes" was sent down – and that evening, advertising changed forever. This unknown, amateur copywriter said to Mr. Thomas…

"Advertising is – Salesmanship in Print."

And, in a time when copywriters were earning $15 per week, John E. Kennedy became the highest paid copywriter on the planet, starting at $28,000 per year. And over the next decade, Chicago became the advertising epicenter of America. Bewildered New York agencies were helpless to stop the flow, as clients defected in mass to this new and powerful advertising form.

And while this definition has never been improved upon, amazingly, it is seldom adhered to. So, what is salesmanship in print? Picture these two events.

1. You walk into pizzeria "A" and ask; "What kind of pizza do you have?" The owner runs back, grabs one out of the oven, rushes back, holds it out in front of you and stands there with a smile on his face. He might even recite some slogan such as *"You've tried the rest – now try the best."*

2. Or, you walk into a pizzeria "B" and ask "What kind of pizza do you have?" And the owner says: "Well, we have the best selling gourmet pizza in the neighborhood. We were voted 'Best Pizza' by the City Weekly. Our meats are fresh, we use whole milk mozzarella, and I personally hand pick and slice every vegetable we use. I'm so confident that you'll love our pizza that I guarantee each one to taste great – or your money back. And, today I'm running a special on our two most popular pizzas. As a matter of fact, I've got one coming out of the oven right now – would you like to see it?"

Which pizza would you buy? Our first example is Image Advertising. Or, "Keeping your name before the public." The second example is pure salesmanship.

Building on this concept, let's return back to that lonely moment in my pizzeria, not far from a botched Formica counter-top, with a cheap pen in my hand.

Squinting out the window through a winter fog, I pondered that question…

"If someone held a gun to my head and told me I needed to get one brand new customer to buy a pizza at full price within 24 hours or they would pull the trigger… what would I do?"

I recognized that if my life was truly "on the line," desperation would be my enemy. People can smell it, like a dog smells fear. I would need to exude passion, excitement and confidence.

And remember, discounting is off the table, so I *need* this prospect to…

1. See that my pizza is clearly a treat like no other

2. Feel an almost desperate urgency to want one right away

3. Understand that the value is so amazing, they'd be a fool to pass on this

With the hammer cocked, and the clock ticking, I would hustle over to the nearest house… knock on the door… and upon someone answering, I'd say;

"Hello neighbor, my name is Kamron and I own Wasatch Pizza right down the street, and I'm here to invite you to stop by and give us a try. Now I certainly realize there are other pizzerias in town. In fact I've eaten at several of them… and they're pretty good. But I'm convinced you and your family will really enjoy our pizza – but since everyone claims to have the "the best pizza in town…" let me take just a minute to tell you what we do different from all the rest.

First of all… we age our pizza dough for several days to bring out the flavor. You know how cheese, wine and beer get better with age? Same thing with dough. It takes time for the yeasts and sugars to interact – ferment and develop a rich complex flavor.

We fold seven pounds of seasonings into each batch of marinara… then slow-simmer it for hours. Then we let it marinate for two days in order for the flavors to saturate. The flavor is out of this world.

A lot of places keep costs down by cutting corners on their cheese… they use a lower-cost skim-milk cheese. You'll never find that on your pizza at my shop… we only use rich whole-milk mozzarella.

Our fresh Italian sausage is never pre-cooked or frozen – it actually cooks right on top of your pizza. We roast whole garlic cloves, hand-cut fresh pineapple and hand-chop fresh rosemary every day.

Anyway, I think you get the idea… but since you've never had our pizza, I realize I'm asking you to take a chance on us. So I'm going to really sweeten the pot here and make this the most tempting offer you've ever heard.

Here's the deal…

If you'll stop by and purchase any large pizza today, I'll give you a loaf of our delicious garlic bread… free. This is made from a very flavorful Foccacia bread slathered with real butter and garlic… then toasted in our oven… you're going to love it. I'd also like to give you one of our Caesar salads. This salad is topped with sun-dried tomatoes, Greek olives and grated parmesan cheese. We make the dressing "in-house" the old fashioned way with real 100% virgin olive oil, red-wine vinegar and real egg yolks. Many have said it's the most delicious salad they've ever had in their life. That of course – is on me as well. Free.

And just to make sure you've got a complete meal – let me throw in a 2-liter bottle of Coke for you too. That way you don't have to worry about grabbing something for the kids to drink. That's free too.

Now… please let me point out that – I stand behind every pizza baked at my shop. If you should ever be disappointed for any reason… just let me know and I'll see that you get a prompt and courteous refund right on the spot. I wouldn't dream of keeping your money if you're not completely thrilled with your pizza. What do you say? Can I count on seeing you tonight for dinner?

Time out: So, let me ask you… With mass-marketing pulling a 1% response rate – if you're lucky, how many doors will I need to knock on to get a taker?

Turns out… less than ten.

Before moving on here though, ask yourself… what just happened?

• A complete sales pitch, pointing out benefits

• A value-added offer (not a discount)

• A money-back guarantee

I didn't just say; "My pizza's the best, buy it from me because I want your money." Instead, I painted a pretty vivid picture which separated me from the others… then I piled on some bonuses… then I took the risk out of trying it – with a guarantee. I never mentioned price.

But I never did knock on a single door. While that would certainly be super effective, you can achieve the same result on a much wider scale. What I did instead was to put that same pitch on paper (salesmanship in print)… and send personalized letters to homes in the neighborhood.

Here's a version of that letter as used by a client…

You be the judge… if this isn't the best pizza you've ever had, I'll give you your money back – every penny! Plus – just for giving us a chance, I'll give you a FREE Garden Salad, FREE Loaf of Garlic Bread, FREE 2-liter bottle of Pepsi, And <u>FREE Delivery</u> when you buy any Large Gourmet Pizza!

Dear Neighbor,

Hi, my name is Kim and I've just opened a great little gourmet pizza store in <u>*your*</u> neighborhood. We make delicious "hand-made" pizza for take-out or **FREE** delivery.

But, since every place claims to have the "best food around" – and even though I have high hopes of earning your trust and confidence – I realize I'm asking you to take a chance on us.

Now, I could tell you all about our fresh roasted garlic, oven roasted peppers, fresh cut rosemary, or our 40 other gourmet toppings – ranging from artichoke hearts to zucchini. **But in the end you have to try it – you have to taste it for yourself. And, that's why I'll do anything I can to get you to try us out.**

So, what I want to do is make you an irresistibly delicious offer – and **<u>I'll take all the risk!</u>**

If I have to give you a **FREE** Garden Salad – I will. If I have to further tempt you with a **FREE** loaf of garlic buttered Foccacia bread – I'll do it! If I have to give you a **FREE** 2-liter bottle of Pepsi to make the meal complete – I'm happy to.

If I have to put my neck on the line with my – iron-clad, money back if you're not absolutely delighted – **<u>100% satisfaction guarantee</u>** – I'll do that too!

So come on, give us a try! Take a look at the menu I sent you – see which one of our designer pizzas gets your mouth watering – then give us a call.

You'll get **FREE** delivery right to your front door – or, you can pick up. You'll find us at 3585 South Durango Dr. Just off of Spring Mountain road – right next to Blockbuster Video. Our phone number is **562-9699**.

And, if our gourmet pizza doesn't live up to your expectations – if it's not what you expected in every way – just let me know. I'll give you your money back. I'd just love for you to give us a try.

Hope to see you soon – sincerely,

Kim

P.S. Please – take us up on this offer tonight! But definitely before Nov. 25t^h. The **FREE** Garlic Bread, **FREE** Garden Salad, **FREE** 2-Liter and **FREE** Delivery are yours – and as always – if you're not 100% satisfied, your money back – every penny!

What you just read doubled my sales in one month. The formatting is a bit different here, versus how it appears on an 8.5 x 11 sheet of paper, but the message is the same. It went out in white envelopes addressed in handwriting font with blue ink, using real spit-stuck stamps. It looked like a personal letter that was meant for you.

The result? Flip the page…

Before...

@Dec 31/00, 09:55 pa   RED ROCK PIZZA ▓▓▓2 ▓▓0 Store 4, Page 1

End—Of—Month report
December 31, 2000

Order type	# of orders	Total dollars	Avg order	% of sales			Running Subtotals
Deliveries	483	8171.67	16.91	62.05%	I Week $		2992.41
Pickups	163	2683.02	16.46	20.37%	I Month $		13169.27
To - Go	209	2284.36	10.92	17.35%	I Year $		14728.68
Eat - In	0	0.00	0.00	0.00%	I Per. $		537.57
Table Orders	6	30.22	5.03	0.23%	I		
Cash Trans	0	0.00	0.00	0.00%	I		
Drive-Thru	0	0.00	0.00	0.00%	I		Running Grand Totals
Subtotal	861	13169.27	15.29	00.00%	I Week $		
Sales tax		954.45			I Month $		14123.72

After...

@Jan 31/01, 10:09 pa   RED ROCK PIZZA ▓▓▓2 ▓▓ Store 4, Page 1

End—Of—Month report
January 31, 2001

Order type	# of orders	Total dollars	Avg order	% of sales			Running Subtotals
Deliveries	1059	19224.00	18.15	70.09%	I Week $		1741.05
Pickups	310	5098.14	16.44	18.59%	I Month $		27428.46
To - Go	285	3106.32	10.89	11.33%	I Year $		27428.46
Eat - In	0	0.00	0.00	0.00%	I Per. $		27966.03
Table Orders	0	0.00	0.00	0.00%	I		
Cash Trans	0	0.00	0.00	0.00%	I		
Drive-Thru	0	0.00	0.00	0.00%	I		Running Grand Totals
Subtotal	1654	27428.46	16.58	00.00%	I Week $		
Sales tax		1990.37			I Month $		29440.83

Orders up 48%... ticket average up by $1.29... and overall sales doubled.

Salesmanship in print is nothing more than your best "gun-to-the-head" sales pitch – converted to print, radio, TV, the web... doesn't matter. No salesman in his right mind would go to a prospect – blurt out some slogan and then just stand there with a goofy grin on his face. And, so it is with advertising. Tell your story. Sell your product.

Burn this into your brain: In the absence of a complete and compelling sales presentation, you have no choice but to compete on price.

I share my discoveries with you now... openly, unhesitatingly, and completely. By the time we're done, when that metaphoric gun is held to your head... you won't even blink.

Force Multiplier

Geneeral Patton said; "No fortress has ever been successfully defended. There is only attack. Attack. And attack some more."

Sticking with the military comparison, defending your business is handled mainly by delivering a consistent product, excellent service and systematically marketing directly to your own customers to hang on to your winnings. These are things you control. However, you are still vulnerable to competitor attacks. Your customers are constantly being enticed to defect to the other side.

The term "Force Multiplier" refers to a dramatic increase in the effectiveness of a particular military force. It adds up the advantages that can give a small force an advantage over a larger force, such as superior position, better weapons, etc.

Therefore, if you and your competitor spend the same on marketing, but their ad pulls a 1/2% response and yours pulls 2%... you'll be acquiring new prospects at one fourth the cost. As a result, you become stronger, they get weaker.

So, even if you don't have deep pockets, doubling, tripling, quadrupling your response rate will multiply the return on your marketing over and above the returns your competitors suffer with. What becomes a necessary cost of mere survival for *them* becomes a wildly lucrative investment for *you*.

An ax in the hands of a skilled lumberjack is one thing. An ax in the hands of a madman is another thing altogether... Tactics without strategy is a battle waged by fools. We turn our attention now, to building a sustainable business and attracting people to it.

Controlling Fire

Marketing is much like fire. It can heat your home and keep you warm. Or it can burn it to the ground... leaving you homeless.

Get very clear on this: Marketing is the *only* area in your business where spending a dollar has the potential to return two, three, four, fifty, or even a hundred. It also carries the potential to evaporate into thin air, or worse... cost you two, or three, or four more dollars in hard cost.

Some will tell you, great marketing will make you rich. That's not true. And I violently disagree... not with the premise... but with the incomplete nature of the statement. That's like a drunk in a bar assuming a beautiful woman will go home with him if only his pick-up line is spot-on. Great marketing will open the conversation. But it's no assurance of business success.

What I see over and over from desperate clients is... a focus on themselves... their need for profit, ease of production and convenient hours of operation – for *them*.

Example: How many times have you received a coupon or offer from a restaurant... gone there to try it, only to find out that in the fine print forbids you to use the offer on Friday, Saturday or holidays?

Now think this through. The restaurant owner knows *they'll* be busy on the weekends and holidays... so *they* don't want to take a chance on losing any revenue during these peak times. They want *you* to adjust your schedule to benefit *them*.

Unfortunately, you show up on Friday night (because you overlooked the "fine print")… get comfortably seated only to get slapped in the face as the waiter tells you your coupon is not valid tonight. You are insulted, slightly embarrassed, and seething with anger.

The focus is on *their* immediate and selfish needs, wants and desires, not yours. And that approach has unintended but catastrophic consequences.

This well-intentioned restaurant owner has unknowingly shot themselves in the foot, increased (not decreased) the ROI of the ad… and made a potential new customer, which was the whole point of running the ad – angry. You may… or may not return.

Let's now "flip" the stage. You arrive on Friday night. The place is busy. You get comfortably seated and present your coupon to the waiter. He presents an enormous smile asks if you've dined here before… you tell him – no, this is our first visit. Your order is taken. The owner of the restaurant then appears at your table, introduces himself… and tells you how thrilled he is that you've stopped by to try the place out, and how pleased he is to meet you. As you're close to finishing your meal… the waiter appears with the dessert tray and tells you to choose whatever catches your eye… because it's "compliments of the owner."

How do you feel now? Special? Important? Welcome? Going to return?

The lifeblood of any business is in the recurring revenue generated by happy, repeat customers who don't need to be chased with expensive advertising. That precious first visit is the equivalent of a first date. You know halfway through… whether there will be a second one.

Likewise, a person makes a subconscious decision to either return to your business or not – during *each* visit they make. The first being absolutely crucial. A misstep here and you've squandered a lifetime of potential revenue.

I found the quickest path to a wildly successful, customer-driven business and the rewards it showered on *me* – was by removing my "owner" hat.

The owner mentality keeps you focused on what's best for you. Unfortunately your customers could care less that you need to make payroll, send a fat check to the government, or pay your rent. They do not care *what they do for you*. With each transaction, they want to know *what you will do for them*.

So, what happens when you create extraordinary marketing that drives thundering herds of traffic your way… and they don't like what they find?

After all… there's nothing like great advertising to murder a bad business…

Money Maze

The rat smells cheese. It's getting closer… oops… not there… over here? Nope. Then it must be around the next corner.

Bingo.

If rats always find the cheese, why can't we? Why do so many business owners keep navigating the same blind alley while expecting different results? Here's the conundrum... Too many business owners don't even recognize how close they are to stumbling across the big one. They suffer a lifetime of heartbreak profits. The result of mediocre marketing on an owner focused business... where just enough cash is generated to keep the lights on, and the doors open. The owner's too broke to move forward and too broke to throw in the towel.

And so, the suicidal tossing of good money after bad continues along three paths... each a dead end. And, the years pass like snails.

Dead end #1. Your marketing is terrible and your business is "owner" focused. This is typical of most business adventures. On a hair-brained whim, someone who "loves to cook..." opens a restaurant. The logic is – the food is so good, no advertising will be needed. That fantasy quickly succumbs to reality and the "We've got the best food in the world" campaign begins. Because the misadventure was under-capitalized to begin with – everything from offers and prices, to quality and consistency revolves around the needs of the frantic owner. Like tying an anchor to their neck as they jump in the pool... they quickly sink to the bottom and stay there until their bank account, equity line and credit cards run dry.

Dead end #2. Your marketing is good, but your business is "owner" focused. Sure, you can pull a crowd. Big deal. Even rotten movies will pull a crowd for a few days until the word gets out. Marketing may keep the lights on and provide a steady little trickle of profit as you lurch from one crisis to the next. But, just like a Ponzi scheme... you eventually run out of victims.

Dead end #3. Your marketing is terrible and your business is "customer" focused. This is the best of the dead-end scenarios. People slowly discover you and over time you build a loyal following. Customer care may win the day – eventually. But real profits are likely to be scarce and you are constantly vulnerable to competition.

Backtrack, make a right or left turn though... and you find yourself in rare company. Your marketing becomes so powerful; your prospects go on a wild ride that only ends when they're at your business with smoke coming out of their wallet. And they can't wait to do it again. Your marketing attracts prospects, and the experience brings them back. Great marketing fills the funnel faster; customer focus generates repeat business and referrals from thrilled customers.

Eyeball these variables, figure out where you fit in and get clear on your direction.

1. Poor marketing simply wastes cash, but luckily, little damage is done to your reputation because few people show up to be disappointed.

2. Good marketing is where it gets dicey. That's because sudden and irreparable damage can be done when huge throngs of eager prospects… leave frustrated or dissatisfied.

3. An owner-focused business, like a spinning top, begins wobbling at some point. At about the third wobble, most owners begin reactively staggering in an ever tightening circle of doom as they blame everything from the weather… to the economy for their predicament. They start discounting with enthusiasm. Oscillating bursts of price-slashing brings ever-diminishing returns. As the discounting high fades and the credit cards get maxed out, marketing stops altogether. After all, for them anyway – marketing doesn't work. Watch for these signs in competitors, because a simple flick of the finger might be all it takes to channel their customers – to you.

4. A customer focused business with great marketing is about as sweet as it gets.

Even lab rats will only go down a dead-end in a maze once or twice before giving up. It's troubling that so many humans, with so much on the line, will often waste a lifetime wandering the same blind alley, refusing to even try a new path. You're not going to be outsmarted by a rat are you?

So, before launching any marketing at all…

Become Your Customer

I attended the Bencivenga 100 Marketing Summit in New York City in May, 2004. This was an amazing once in a lifetime event and attendance was limited to 100 guests. I considered myself fortunate to be rubbing shoulders with the top marketers in the world. The three-day event was taught by Gary Bencivenga, widely regarded as the most brilliant (and expensive) copywriter in the world. Gary shared a story at this event that encapsulates the premise of what you'll discover in these pages. The essence of the story is this: An individual fisherman on a rinky-dink boat hauls in more fish than tricked-out commercial boats.

His name is Captain John Rade, and he's a commercial fisherman in Montauk, New York. He's famous out there too, because on most days, John brings in more fish by himself, than boats carrying 50 or 60 fishermen. He doesn't use big nets, fancy gear, or lines with hundreds of baited hooks either. When asked by a local reporter, what his secret was… John said; "Don't think like a fisherman, think like a fish."

His perspective is unique. Rather than hunt fish on his terms… he attracts them on theirs. He doesn't get caught up on the latest toys, gimmicks or gadgets. He understands the fish, knows where they'll be, and what they bite on.

Your shortcut to success too, is not based on "angles" or hard to find "secret knowledge." It is based on common, simple sense. Become your customer… walk in their shoes… think their thoughts… solve their problems. Experience your business – *as they do.*

Park across the street or far out in the parking lot. Look around. What do you see? Do you notice trash? Potholes? How's the paint? Windows clean? Sign working?

Inside… is it neat and clean? No, I mean really clean. Is there grime around the baseboards? How are the bathrooms? Carpet? Lighting?

These impressions begin building as each customer transacts business with you. What must you do to make each customer "feel" important and special?

Each contact point from the parking lot to the greeting to the inter-action to the follow-up is a marketing opportunity. You'll never experience the full potential of your business until you take a walk in your customer's shoes. I suggest you try on a pair and evaluate the fit – at once.

I wrote this column for Pizza Today magazine. It ought to be a bit of an eye-opener.

Do me a favor... check your mailbox at the pizzeria... hmmmnnn... what's that? A letter from a customer?

April 5, 2008

From John & Jane Doe

To YOUR Pizzeria

We'd like to tell you something you might not be aware of... since the economy's been a little tough lately, we've scaled back on going out to fancy restaurants... but we still want to treat ourselves – and pizza is an affordable and fun meal for the family. And for that reason, we're actually getting pizza more often – now that things are a little tight.

But just the other night when we stopped by, we noticed a sun-faded, grimy picture hanging on the wall. It used to be bright and beautiful. A pile of tacky lemon-yellow flyers were bunched up next to the cash register. A tell-tale sign of desperation. The table wobbles. It was quite distracting as my family wrestled with it during our entire meal.

And there's something else that's somewhat troubling... if your kitchen looks anything like the bathroom... we are truly frightened.

Also, on the way over here we saw that new pizzeria down the street. Have you seen it? It's shiny as a new penny. Their advertising talks of dough made with spring harvest flour. Sauce that's loaded with seasonings and marinated for hours. Premium whole-milk mozzarella. Sounds pretty tasty.

Do you have that stuff? I can't remember if you've ever told me – now that I think about it.

Anyway, listen – we've been ordering from you for years and we don't mean to be rude – but if you don't wake up and get it together we're going to try that new place down the block.

Signed,

John & Jane

Now, hopefully that letter got dropped in the wrong mailbox and was really intended for the pizzeria down the street. But, let's make sure…

Go down to your pizzeria early in the morning when it's quiet – before anyone shows up, with paper and pen in hand – and do a thorough walk-through. See it through the eyes of your customers. Replace the faded picture. Clean the corners with a toothbrush. Fix that wobbly table.

Then, re-examine your current marketing strategy. And remember, if you don't compete on your product, your only choice is to compete on price. Remind your customers of the value they gain from choosing you. Paint a vivid picture of the premium ingredients and amazing taste. And do not – trim your marketing budget. It's a rookie mistake that will cost you far more in the long run, than it will save you today.

No doubt, the economy is tough right now. It's tough every where… not just your town. Flour, cheese, and labor are digging into your pocket. Gas prices are affecting costs across the board. Still, you have customers who believe in you. You're already doing a lot of things right.

Crawl into the head of John & Jane Doe… and look at your place through *their* eyes.

So, let me ask you: If your life depended on getting each customer to return for a second, third, or fourth visit… how would you treat them? What would you do differently than you're doing now?

Gun to the head marketing begins with a "customer" focused message. It's not you they want to hear about – but themselves. You're not the star of the ad – they are.

Movie Stars & Money

If you were given the opportunity to be in a big movie, would you prefer to be the leading character, or a stand-in? Would you prefer close-up shots where your face blasts onto the screen bigger than life, or would you rather be a speck in the distance? Well, there's the problem. We all want to be the "star." So, even when we're creating a new ad – it's all about us.

Our logo is screaming across the top of the ad. Man it looks great. We blather on about how great our product is… in fact: "It's the best in town." And we arrogantly assume that everyone who sees this ad will be mesmerized by our greatness. They'll study each word as though in a state of rapture. They'll marvel at how extraordinary we are.

Wake up. Truth is, when people are handed a ballpoint pen to try out in a store, they write their name, not yours. When looking at a map, people look for their hometown or their house, not yours. And when eyeballing a photo of them – and others, they study themselves the most.

Each individual is the star of their own life. Sure, others are on the stage, and friends and family members share the limelight. But don't for a minute think you're a welcome part of the scene. You are allowed on stage when needed for the plot. Your job is to create a stage where your prospect can bask in the spotlight. Your message is not about you, it's about them.

Most ads are a study in arrogance. From now on, you operate the spotlight. Your prospect basks in the warm glow. They are the star.

Mind Control

It seems as though the purpose of our new brain, is to satisfy the desires of our ancient brain.

You open your eyes; cock your ear – and the world rushes in. You, me, everyone… lives the entire amazing human experience in the cramped eight inches between each ear. Your entire life is contained in the very tiny coconut-sized cavern of your skull.

About three pounds and several thousand miles of interconnected nerve cells (about 100 billion) control every thought and experience you will ever have.

And bathed in a rich chemical soup, our upper brains are divided into two very dissimilar factions. The right side is emotional and makes all the decisions. The left side is logical, and hunts for reasons to let the right side have its way. It's a blend of facts and feelings.

And picture this; unless you could file away and store experiences – everything would be *new* all the time. You could never learn or make sense of anything. You would be overwhelmed. You would be forced to think about everything. So, things that are repeated often – get chemically filed away for easy recall. Repetition slowly converts electrical fragments to chemical bonds. This wiring and chemistry creates habits. Constant repetition associated with feelings, ego gratification or outcomes builds a solid bridge from impulse to product. It eliminates or at least shortcuts the decision-making process. We don't think, we just *do*. This is the world of *branding*. And, it's what causes someone to reach for the Del Monte instead of the less-expensive house brand. It just *feels* right.

But that's just half the story. You know how thoughts seem to pop into your head from time to time? Where do you think they come from? Your subconscious has been puzzling over the name of that one actor dude that played a mobster in a movie. And bingo… three days later the name pops into your head while you're clipping your nails.

Your limbic system… the ancient lizard brain, just under that wrinkly part of your brain, is run by a committee of specialists. They stay busy making sense of the world around you, and occasionally throw something upstairs for further review.

So, by the time a thought or desire pops into your consciousness, your limbic system (the ancient lower brain) has already taken a look at it. In fact… that's "why" it pops into your "mind." A particular desire has already aroused interest, and now it is served up to your conscious mind for evaluation. That begins the fight as emotions collide with logic. "I really want that 60-inch Plasma TV. It looks crazy-awesome. But, it costs $2,700… and I really should put that money in the bank… then again, what will my friends think when they come over for the game next week and all I've got is this stupid old 35-incher?" And so you find yourself backing out of the driveway for the short journey to Best Buy.

Science has shown that electrical activity begins in the subconscious prior to manifesting itself in the "self aware" conscious mind. Desires are simply passed to us for our opinion.

This "emotion versus facts" most likely evolved so we could have some say in how we allocated scarce resources in an uncertain world. It gives us infinite survival scenarios, whereas rabbits are just hard-wired to run for their lives. These two opposing forces actually force us to "think." "I want it, but what are the consequences?" "What will it cost me?" "Does the pleasure outweigh the price?"

So, our epic challenge as marketers is to momentarily interrupt the prospects routine, gain focused attention, and encourage the committee in the ancient brain to alert the upper brain. Then, to bring a decision into balance.

So picture the brain for a minute, as though it were a castle surrounded by a forbidding moat. As you approach, a guard shouts down; "Who goes there… what do you want?"

And you say; "I'm here to sell the King some arrows for his armory." "The King has plenty of arrows… go away or I'll put one of them in your neck."

The guard rebuffs you without so much as even checking with the King.

Imagine though, if you'd said; "There are 3,000 angry peasants brandishing torches and weapons just fifteen minutes behind me. And they're in a hurry. They said something about capturing the castle and murdering everyone inside – including the King. Now, I just happen to have a few thousand arrows here that are twice as accurate, and fly three times farther than the ones you currently use. You can easily repel these goons before they pose any threat to the King. Shall I come in so you can see for yourself, before the murderous mob arrives?"

Most likely, this information will get kicked upstairs to the King. Fast too.

So, as electrical signals flash through a dense thicket of nerve cells bringing news from the outside world… our guards stand duty. The gate is lowered – only for friends bearing valuable news. The more this news stimulates our emotional wants… the more we pay attention.

So, given a rare audience with the King… here's what you'll want to know: Language is processed mainly in the brain's left hemisphere. But words containing an emotional component are processed in *both* hemispheres. And words processed for emotion, create feelings (this is very important and what most of your marketing will revolve around). Of interest – women tend to process language on both sides of the brain. They also wire up and react to emotional memories more actively than men do (they also control most of the spending).

Market first to the emotions, while providing plenty of facts for the modern brain to ratify the decision.

Ads featuring heroes like Michael Jordon wire us directly to the product by ego association. We are cool and more like our hero while donning their footwear. We become gourmet chefs while cooking with Emeril's cookware.

AT&T took advantage of this in TV commercials years ago. Mom was at home all alone. The phone rings, she answers it – and bang! Her son is on the line and mom is all happy now. They associated their service with being a caring child and making mom happy. What's remarkable is that AT&T measured a significant spike in long distance phone calls within minutes of those commercials hitting the airwaves (mainly on Sunday evening).

One of the most popular and remembered TV ads in history is the Coca Cola "I'd like to teach the world to sing" commercials. It was a "feel good" message. You associated Coke with feeling wonderful. And people naturally gravitate to things they associate with the warm fuzzies.

Think about it this way… you don't have to *think* about sticking your hand on a hot stove. You've associated that with pain. You don't have to *think* about cuddling up next to a warm fire on a cold day, you associate that with pleasure.

This is subliminal association. Linking feelings to your product. You'll fast-track your sales by tapping into this already established mental architecture. Here's what you need to know:

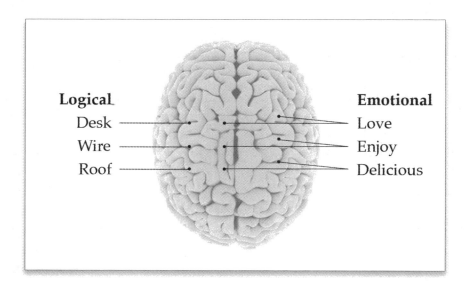

We've all heard that a picture is worth a thousand words. Likewise, carefully chosen words – can paint not only a vivid picture, but even a mental movie.

Remember, generic non emotional words get processed for literal meaning in the left (logical) side of the brain – only. Words with an emotional component get processed in both sides. And since we buy things based on feelings... it is the feelings we need to stir.

Test yourself:

1. "Come buy and eat my pizza."

Did that get you salivating? Did you visualize a fun experience? Try this...

2. "Now, you can delight your whole family with Red Rock Pizza. They'll enjoy hot, delicious pizza – made from the finest hand selected vegetables and the freshest, juiciest meats. And, you'll be thrilled with our low, family-friendly prices."

Now, the funny thing is – they both essentially "say" the same thing. But the first one falls flat as a pancake. The second one though creates theatre of the mind; a significant distinction. The words; Delight, family, enjoy, delicious, hand-selected, freshest, juiciest, thrilled, and friendly... paint subtle, subconscious pictures. Delighting your family (quick flash in the mind's theatre). Enjoying the pizza (another flash). Thrilled at the family-friendly prices (icing on the cake). These still-frames produce your movie. We are drawn towards pleasure.

In fact, every time you've wandered into a Costco you've seen the pleasure pumps at work.

Big screen TVs and electronic gadgets fascinate us. They cause a burst of dopamine to saturate the pleasure center of the brain. So, you're already feeling good as you grip the cart. Then you find candy and chocolate and tasty samples strategically throughout. At almost every turn, there's something to prime your pleasure center. On top of that, the warehouse atmosphere along with "Hot Buy" and "Super Saver" signage reinforces our perception of everything being a "good deal."

They strategically "put" you in a pleasurable state as you navigate the isle… filling your enormous cart.

Understanding how to slide in under the radar, project a mental movie, and trigger emotion… is transformational. Our real job as marketers is to sharpen desire and connect it to pleasure.

Phineas Gage

Phineas Gage was the foreman of a railway construction gang working for the contractors preparing the bed for the Rutland and Burlington Rail Road near Cavendish, Vermont. On September 13, 1848, an accidental explosion of a charge he had set – blew a tamping iron through his head.

The tamping iron was over 3 feet long and weighed 13 pounds. The iron rod went in point first under his left cheek bone right behind his left eyeball and continued on through the two hemispheres of the cortex and completely out through the top of his skull, landing about 25 yards behind him. Man-o-man was it a mess!

And what a way to ruin your day. Anyway, as luck would have it… Phineas recovered quit nicely from his little mishap – with one exception… he had the most difficult time making decisions.

He would literally be paralyzed when faced with something as simple as what to have for breakfast. What to wear. Where to go.

They didn't know "why" then. They do now. His emotional wiring had been ripped out. And, an emotional "anchor" is required to make a decision in 96% of the human population. (Psychopaths can't access emotion.)

Almost every decision we make is run through a "cost/benefit" analysis. A decision is then made when we decide that the benefit outweighs the cost. To us, costs are money, time, hassle, effort, inconvenience, etc. Benefits are pleasure. Such as, a great meal, a new car, a nice vacation, etc.

Our analytical left brain sorts through the "cost" part. Our emotional right brain compares that to the pleasure or benefit we will receive. So, there you have it – when the benefit outweighs the cost – a decision is made to take action.

This is significant because most of your competitors are just screaming about their "price." Price is not a benefit. The only thing that is a benefit is the "pleasure" we get from the product when we are using it.

Crack open your readers' subconscious minds and make them see exactly what you want them to see. Feel what you want them to feel. Do… what you want them to do.

Triple Threat

How many grains of sand on the earth? I don't have the foggiest idea. How many dollars in circulation? No idea. How many ways are there to grow your business? Three. Exactly three.

There's a mind-numbing number of complex theories, and speculation about how to get a business off the launch pad and into a high financial orbit. But guess what? It all boils down to this:

There are three ways – and only three ways to grow any business.

They are:

1. Increase the average sale. (Up-Selling)

2. Increasing purchase frequency. (Work Your Existing Customers)

3. Increase the number of customers. (Acquire New Customers)

Now, any one of these alone will increase your sales and profits. Work all three as an ongoing system and you'll find yourself on a magic carpet ride.

The 10% Solution

Many owners become frozen with indecision... growing sales and profit seems as unachievable as a three-minute mile. Just getting through the day seems to be figuring out what crisis to attend to first. But unless you focus and get started, unless you change something... the next ten years are likely to be exactly like the last ten, or worse.

We already know there are only three ways to grows sales. What if we set out to boost each one by just ten percent? Doesn't seem unattainable does it? We'll attract more customers. Give them repeated and continual reasons to visit more often. And we'll offer specials and value-added bundles encouraging them to eagerly spend more money with you.

Let's do a little marketing for...

Business "X"

Business "X" has 1000 customers who purchase 12 times a year, and spend $12 each visit. That comes out to $144,000 a year in gross sales. Okay, let's turn up the heat a little.

10 + 10 + 10 = $47,664 – is that right? Can't be. Hmmm... must be that new math they're talking about. Let's investigate further.

Lookey here: A simple increase of 10% across-the-board means we have:

- **1100 customers instead of 1000.**

- **An average sale of $13.20 instead of $12.00**

- **13.2 purchases per year instead of 12**

But the best part is that sales went from $144,000 to a whopping $191,644, a gain of $47,664.

Did I ask Business "X" to do anything crazy? Not at all. If anything, this seems a bit modest, but would an extra $47,000 come in handy? Scale those numbers up to whatever your current sales are. And by all means, 10% is just an example; you're free to haul bigger truckloads of cash to the bank if the mood strikes you.

Let's recap: Marketing is the only activity in your business that has the power to generate revenue. Everything else is an expense. A customer-focused business naturally stands the best chance of dominating any niche.

There are three ways to grow your business and even small increases in each area can mean the difference between rocketing out of obscurity – or not.

What follows is not trickery, hypnotism, or manipulation. The techniques you're about to see will help you cut the fog of competition right down the middle and convey a vast ocean of benefits to your prospects.

We're ready to get into the nitty-gritty now...

Attract More Customers

I f your life absolutely depended on getting someone to purchase from you at full price within the next 24 hours, what would you do? How would you get them to almost uncontrollably demand that you hand over your product, and take their money?

Strategy: Rather than see customers as a resource to be plundered, you'll view them as friends to be looked after, protected, appreciated, and respected. You'll build your business and marketing so as to *attract* them instead of constantly chasing after them.

Therein lays the magic. Once someone has decided to purchase from you, and they've come to that conclusion on their own… it is all but impossible to stop them.

In this section:

• See how a well-crafted message brings clarity to you, while creating doubt about your competitors.

• Discover a simple, easy to remember four-step formula that forces you to create powerful ads.

• Learn how to gain the attention of your prospects, capture their interest, and gain their trust.

• Find out how to combine proven techniques into winning ads that outperform the dribble your competitors crank out.

• Gain the confidence to stare down any competitor, confront any threat, and fight any battle.

It boils down to this: Value is a perception. People trade what they value *less*… for what they value *more*.

The task to which we now turn to is how to take control of attracting and acquiring new customers by controlling perceptions.

Message Control

Picture yourself at the Super Bowl. The stadium's packed. Your team is winning. And, life is good. Halftime hits and you're just about ready to head to the snack bar for a beer when – out of the corner of your eye –you notice some dude making a beeline – straight for you.

As it turns out – you've been secretly chosen for the opportunity of a lifetime. With Super Bowl ads selling at $2.4 million each – YOU will have the chance to "pitch" your pizzeria to a nationwide audience for free – right now.

Your mind is whirling as you're led to the 50-yard line. A microphone is stuffed in your hand and the announcer says; "For the first time in Super Bowl history – we've picked an average Joe from our audience to deliver a live 60-second commercial… so here's Bob from Bob's Pizza – take it away Bob!"

The crowd grows quiet. All eyes are on you. The camera swings around, and the director counts down… 3, 2, 1, GO! You stare into the camera, a bead of sweat trickles down your forehead, and the director is silently mouthing "your on, we're live." You're frozen in terror – your mind erupting in a jumbled torrent of unconnected mish-mash.

And finally, a pasty-faced you mumbles… "I own Bob's Pizza. We have the best pizza in town. Oh yah – we also make dough fresh daily – and we use real cheese."

As you stagger off the field your thoughts are racing. Certainly the "best pizza" thing will get them coming in. If not that – the part about using "real cheese" will do the trick. But somehow – this time, you realize the emptiness of what you just said. *You blew it big time.* Because, as it stands – the rudderless dribble you just poured into the microphone has only cemented your membership in the "My pizza is better than yours" club. An incredibly overcrowded association with staggering financial dues.

Today though, the halftime debacle has shifted you're thinking. No longer will you be put on the spot – stumbling and mumbling. No. It's finally sunk in… the enormity of what you do for your customers. The benefits they gain by choosing you. The great care and expense you put into every pizza – to make it the best they could ever have.

Starting now, you will craft a clear, concise message – void of the typical gibberish. You will articulate, very specifically what separates your pizzeria from your competitors – after all, the very first step to eliminating your competition is to separate yourself from them.

Like: "When it absolutely, positively has to be there overnight." Or, "Better Ingredients. Better Pizza." Or, "Tylenol, the pain reliever Doctors use most."

These concise messages are commonly called USPs, unique selling propositions. People rely on these little messages to help them choose. After all, if it's the one Doctors choose most… that saves you from having to figure out which pain reliever to buy.

Likewise, your advertising and marketing must present a recurring theme. A consistent message. A message that leads back to you.

I still get calls to this day from clients telling me how well the "Million Dollar Letter" pulls in new prospects – and brings back lost customers. This full-page letter, explains in vivid detail – what is offered to the prospect, and why it is different from the competition.

It fills up an entire 8.5 X 11 page. It never mentions price either. Instead, it creates desire. It focuses the prospect on what they "get" not what they "pay." And, it controls and limits the prospects critical thinking (which is dangerous when you're trying to persuade).

That's because, if you allow a prospect to fill in the "blank" spaces in an ad with their own preconceived notions… they will NOT pay a dollar more for your product than they will for another. That's because you've allowed *them* to define *your* product – with their perception of what it should be. Not necessarily what it *is*.

If they don't know you use premium ingredients, top-of-the-line parts, or advanced techniques, if you don't point that out to them… all they see is a "regular" product.

If they don't know your pizza or widget is 30% bigger than your competitors… guess what? They'll assume yours is the same size as the last one they bought.

That's because when your prospect encounters gaps in the information they're receiving from your ad – they have a stunning tendency to fill in those gaps with their own ideas. In other words: They just make it up as they go. And you lose control of your message when this happens. You become a prisoner of their preexisting perceptions.

Here's a concrete example: "Do you prefer the taste of whole-roasted garlic cloves, garden-fresh, hand-chopped rosemary and fresh (bakes right on your pizza) Italian sausage… over the "fast-food" powders, flakes and mystery meat? If you do, you're going to love Angelina's Pizza… and here's an offer that's sure to put a smile on your face… and it starts with an extra large pizza that's *more* than big enough to satisfy the whole family…"

Gonna get everybody in the front door? No. Just the exact people you WANT! It tells bargain-hunters to stay away. That's because you're not pointing at a "price." You are instead bringing the focus to your "point of distinction…" fresh, premium ingredients, on a "big" pizza.

Merely screaming "best, cheapest, fastest" allows prospects to sniff suspiciously at your proposal and paint your offering with their own brush. Those outlandish claims have lost their power. They mean… nothing.

If your "customers" don't automatically think of you when needing what you have to offer… you've failed to paint a vivid, colorful image of the benefits you provide.

So, if you jimmied some locks and snuck into a few of your customers' homes at three in the morning, woke each one from a sound sleep and asked them to describe what's special about your business... you want each one to say nearly the same thing.

People hate a void. And in the absence of that void being filled by you... they will fill in the blanks themselves. You simply can't count on thousands of prospects figuring out on their own – what you do different, and why they should care. That's your job. You need to paint a complete picture, every brushstroke.

Persuasion Equation

Earlier we discovered that "Advertising is salesmanship in print." And fortunately, salesmanship can be broken down into identifiable steps...

One of the most difficult things you can do is to stare down at a blank page and realize that your task is to create an ad that will sell your product... an ad that will drive traffic... an ad that will bring back a return on the investment. And the real cost of an ineffective or mediocre ad is more devastating than just the cost of placing it. The cost of placing an ad is one thing... the loss you suffer when the ad doesn't produce cash-in-hand customers – is another.

Thankfully, since the late 1800s a handful of advertising pioneers have tested and tweaked thousands of ads and compiled a catalog of variables and how they affect response rates. They've solved such mysteries as:

- What kind of headlines attract the most readers?

- What kind of pictures gain the most attention?

- What sales appeal sells the most product?

- What kind of ad copy is most effective?

Here's what they've discovered…

• Headlines promising a benefit or a news angle out-pull all others

• Photographs showing the product in use are the best

• Appeals based on emotion and backed up by facts… are sure-fire

• Conversational "slang" copy, out-pulls grammatically correct copy

A print ad consists of two components; copy and layout. Let's tackle copy first. This is the meat of your ad.

And here's a proven, step-by-step system you can follow to achieve the greatest response and profit possible from your advertising copy. It all begins by crawling into your prospect's head and getting in step with *their* internal thinking process. People (all of us) first have a want – or desire. We then look for something that promises to satisfy that desire. Of the available options – we gravitate to the one that proves or guarantees to deliver on that promise and seems to deliver the most value, or bang for the buck.

Gary Bencivenga, the lavishly-paid "super copywriter" I mentioned earlier, has a nifty little formula he uses, and it's easy to remember. He calls it the "Persuasion Equation." Problem + Promise + Proof + Proposition = Persuasion.

Problem

People are seeking to solve a problem. They're hungry and want a meal – in a hurry. The top three motivators are: Fast (they want it now). Cheap (they want the lowest price they can find). Delicious (they want a tasty meal – and will pay for it).

And don't confuse needing a meal with needing a pizza – from you. Four dollar pizzas are sitting in the grocery store cold-case – right next to Wolfgang Puck's gourmet stuff. Options are endless.

Promise

Promise nothing and you become vulnerable to a competitor. Promise low prices and you will attract hordes of budget conscious coupon clippers. Promise a mouth watering pizza – and you will attract those who value taste over price.

Proof

Several ways to do this… use a guarantee or a photograph or testimonials.

- "The tastiest pizza you've ever had or your money back"
- "We guarantee to take any competitors' coupons"
- "30-minute delivery – or your pizza is free"

Photographs are great at conveying proof. If you're selling a high-end gourmet pizza – invest in the most mouth watering photo you can get. Blow it up and make it the focal point of your ad. Three pizzas for $10 each? Then show three pizzas. Fast delivery? Show the driver handing the pizza to a mom right at the front door.

And from infomercials to book covers, we rely on the opinions of others to help guide us to a comfortable decision. We'll cover this in more detail soon.

Proposition

This is your offer. I'm not big on discounting to begin with, and a recent study confirms that 66% of shoppers are NOT seeking the lowest price. They are seeking value. They just want to get their "money's worth." I've found that adding free items with a high "perceived value" – not only pulls very well, but attracts the kind of people that are likely to repurchase without a coupon.

So, immediately present your prospect with a problem that's bugging them. Promise to solve the problem. Prove that *you* can do this (better, faster, cheaper, more effectively than competitors). Then make an irresistible proposition that's impossible to pass up.

So, in the pizza world most ads merely state that they have pizza, and quickly default to the price… "Large Pizza Only $9.99." As a smart marketer, your ad would say" Best pizza you've ever had or your money back. Plus you'll get a FREE 2-Liter, FREE Salad, and FREE loaf of Garlic Bread when you order a Large Pizza.

So, both ads offer to solve a problem. Both will provide you a pizza. But the second ad promises a great tasting pizza, proves that claim with a guarantee, and then instead of discounting the price – they do a compelling value-added offer.

Another variation is *AIDA*. This acronym stands for: Attention, Interest, Desire, Action. All successful ads pretty much stick with this flow. After all, if your life depends on your ad getting read… it needs to attract attention. Generate interest. Fuel desire for your product. And have a strong call to action that generates a purchase.

A problem-solving, attention-getting ad is the equivalent of minting money. So let's discover how to command immediate attention.

Headless Body in Topless Bar

Jay Abraham coined the phrase: "The headline is the ad, for the ad." And a headline is not just in print. The first sentence in a radio or T V spot is essentially a headline. The subject line in an email is a headline. The opening sentence of a sales letter is a headline. A pay-per-click ad on Google is a headline.

The New York Post has written some of the catchiest headlines ever. On par with the National Enquirer. There's actually a book out that chronicles 200 years of headlines.

Now think about this… would anybody bother to plow through a newspaper if there were no headlines? We rely on headlines to quickly convey things of importance to us. Sports scores, stock quotes, the latest murder.

I mean, what if you saw the following headline in the morning paper?

In 1497, 16-year-old Lucrezia Borgia Became Pregnant.
The Result of an Incestuous Affair Inside the Vatican –
With Her Father – the Pope!

Does that have stopping power or what? It just keeps building until its shocking and stunning end. It's so outrageous (and true) that you'd be hard-pressed not to read that story. In fact, I'll bet I can get you to read a 500 page book by just crafting a single headline… "This Book is all About (Your Name Here)." But what if I said: "This Book is all About Me?"

In fact David Ogilvy of the famous "Ogilvy & Mather" Advertising Agency said: "On average, five times as many people read headlines as read body copy. It follows that, unless your headline sells your product, you have wasted 90 percent of your money."

Let's write some headlines.

We'll work on a headline for your one-year anniversary. You're going to give out free pizza all day to boost awareness of your store.

Here's the first idea for a headline:

It's Our 1-Year Anniversary And We're Giving Away
Free Pizza All Day This Saturday

It conveys the message. But, I have to start with the boring word "It's." Followed by "our." Remember, people want to know "what's in it for me." So, using "our" makes 2 weak words in a row.

For the most part, the headline is full of filler. And, it's in the "passive" voice.

Passive voice – "Here's why many customers have enjoyed eating our Grilled Salmon."

Active voice – "Here's why many customers *enjoy eating* our Grilled Salmon."

Passive voice – "People have enjoyed our Eggs Benedict."

Active voice – "People *enjoy* our Eggs Benedict."

We want action, so always write actively.

How about:

**We're Giving Away Free Pizza All Day This Saturday
for Our 1-Year Anniversary.**

It's a little zippier, but still very flat. What else can we cut?

We're Giving Away Free Pizza All Day This Saturday.

We're getting close. In fact, there are only 3 words that mean anything here. They are:

• Free, Pizza, Saturday

Free Pizza All Day Saturday!

Now, that will get some attention. So will this:

Announcing – Free Pizza all Day Saturday!

We've gone from:

**It's Our 1-Year Anniversary And We're Giving Away
Free Pizza All Day This Saturday**

To: **"Announcing – Free Pizza all Day Saturday!"**

The first headline strayed from the basic premise of a good headline. It wasn't an ad for the ad. *It was the ad*. The final example is clean and to the point. A quick glance tells you all you need to know – to decide if you'll look at the rest of the ad.

The body copy is where you give the details. Not the headline.

This is one of the headlines I used to sell the Black Book Marketing System.

**"This Week You Can Learn
Every Trick, Tactic, Secret and
Shortcut That I Personally Used to
Explode Sales in My Pizzeria by
$27,000 a Week..."**

*The astonishing story behind one of the
most amazing pizza turnarounds in history...*

If you owned a pizzeria and wanted to increase sales... that's most likely going to get your attention.

John Carlton is by far the headline King. That guy has written some of the most throat-grabbing headlines I've ever seen. This is one of his most famous:

Amazing Secret Discovered By One-Legged Golfer Adds 50 Yards To Your Drives, Eliminates Hooks And Slices... And Can Slash Up To 10 Strokes From Your Game Almost Overnight!

John loves to bring in a hook that stops you dead in your tracks. And as you'll notice, he also piles on not one, not two, but three benefits.

- **Adds 50 yards...**
- **Eliminates hooks...**
- **Slashes 10 strokes...**

John has mastered the three-benefit headline.

Years ago, I pulled advertising banners with my airplane. It was then that I began to really focus of crafting a concise, powerful message. That's because you're limited to just seven or eight words on an aerial banner.

Visual Gulps

Eyeballs scan… looking for things of interest. When they spot something, they'll hesitate and focus for a second. So, a neat little trick is to "stack" your headlines so that key words are easily spotted in the visual gulp areas. Look again at our first headline…

It's Our 1-Year Anniversary And We're Giving Away Free Pizza All Day This Saturday.

Putting the key word "Free" clear over at the end of the first line hides it a bit. But by moving it down and making it the first word on the second line, we increase its stopping power.

It's Our 1-Year Anniversary And We're Giving Away Free Pizza All Day This Saturday.

Once you've chosen the KEY words for your headline, you may need to stack the headline to get those key words out into the "visual gulp" area. People gulp down several words at a time. So, once they've managed to haphazardly glance at your ad – the key words need to be "out" in plain sight. Not buried in the middle. Here are some examples:

This one looks good either way.

Buy One Get One FREE.

Buy One Get One FREE.

Definitely better stacked.

Two Pizzas for the Price of One.

Two Pizzas For the Price of One.

Better stacked.

Large 1-Topping Pizza Only 9.99.

Large 1-Topping Pizza Only 9.99.

Stack this one for sure.

Large 3-Topping Pizza Only 12.99 Plus, FREE Breadsticks, and FREE 2- Liter.

Large 3-Topping Pizza Only 12.99 Plus...
FREE Breadsticks
FREE 2- Liter

The last example really illustrates the importance of stacking. The three hot button words are all buried in the middle – out of the quick-glance visual gulp area.

When stacked – "Plus, FREE, FREE" – jump out.

Words at the beginning and the end of your headline are recalled more easily than words in the middle. Get the "key" words out on the edges.

Start or end each line with a key word. Play around with stacking until your headline practically reads itself to you.

Got news for you too. The most powerful word in marketing is not "free." It is "you."

This small ad I created for Aircraft Tool Supply uses "FREE" as the hook… but then we immediately put the reader "in" the ad. The word you – makes the message personal.

Every ad you create goes into one set of eyeballs and one mind at a time.

• This offer is for **YOU**.

• This steak is for **YOU**.

• These toppings are for **YOU**.

• I work my butt off all day to make **YOU** a great chicken dinner.

• This special is for **YOUR** family.

Put the name of the community in the headline: **Salt Lake's #1 Selling Gourmet Pizza.**

This also makes it very personal. People identify with their hometown. The less personal your ad – the LESS impact it will have. Load your advertising with **YOU!**

The 10 most powerful headline words are: You, your, how, new, who, free, now, people, want and why.

Also, the human mind – must know what is new. It is hardwired into our genes. Survival depended on it eons ago. We're a curious bunch. New things could deeply affect our lives, so we had to pay attention. Just last night I noticed a tube of Crest toothpaste at the store. It said:

NEW LOOK!
Same product.

So, even when they don't have a "new" product – they scream about a NEW look.

Pizza Hut has been playing the "New" card for years. I doubt anyone can recall all the new things they've thrown at us over the years. But, you can count on it. Once a year they'll roll out some "NEW" product, and advertise it like crazy.

Then, after a while, once the "Newness" has worn off – they dump it. But, boy does it make the phones ring!

Now – <u>YOU</u> can get <u>Salt Lake's</u> #1 Selling Gourmet Pizza!

The headline above has New (Now), You (Home town), and Crowd Approval – (#1 selling). I'm sure YOU can come up with something NEW.

We're a curious species… "new" things penetrate our minds.

• **NEW Breadsticks!**

• **NEW Pizzas!**

• **NEW Toppings!**

• **NEW Baby-back Ribs!**

• **NEW Banana Pancakes!**

And **FREE** can't be beat as an eyeball stopper. Free, will serve you well as a "value added" approach.

• **FREE Appetizer with any Entree**

• **FREE 2-Liter with any Large Pizza**

• **FREE Salad with any Dinner**

• **FREE Wine with any Entrée**

• **FREE Unlimited Drink Re-fills w/Dinner**

Heck, why not use all three? **YOU** get a **FREE** Appetizer with any **NEW** Entree!

Always capitalize, bold, and enlarge the word **FREE**. Let's put together some more headlines using our Power Headline words.

• **Announcing**: 7 All **New** Fajitas!

• **Presenting** – The **NEW** Triple Pepperoni Pizza!

• **Who** Else Wants **FREE** Dessert!

• **Now You** Get **FREE** Delivery!

• **Introducing** – The **NEW** Meat Lover Pizza!

- **NOW** – The **Biggest** Steak in Town, **Yours** at Half Price!

- **Why You** Get **More** Pizza For Less **Money** at Randy's Pizza.

- **Which** One of These Great Tasting Pizzas Do **YOU Want – Tonight?**

These headlines command attention. They've got zip, and a news feel to them.

The word "**Anniversary**" tests very well with women. (I wonder why?) And, you'll notice that Papa John's has an "Anniversary" promo every year, usually during 1st quarter. Maybe you should, too.

Let's add some punch to this headline.

You'll Get the Best Pizza You've Ever Had
Prices You Haven't Seen Since 1980
Plus, You'll Get FREE Delivery in Less Than 32 Minutes!

All bolded…

You'll Get the Best Pizza You've Ever Had
Prices You Haven't Seen Since 1980
Plus, You'll Get FREE Delivery in Less Than 32 Minutes!

Key Words **Bold**…

You'll Get the Best Pizza **You've** Ever Had
Prices **You** Haven't Seen Since 1980
Plus, **You'll** Get **FREE** Delivery in Less Than 32 Minutes!

Underlining, FREE Larger Type…

You'll Get the <u>Best Pizza</u> **You've** Ever Had
Prices **You** Haven't Seen Since 1980
<u>*Plus,*</u> **You'll** Get **FREE** Delivery in <u>Less Than 32 Minutes!</u>

Your headline will make, or break your ad. Your ad costs the same – whether one person reads it or 100 people read it.

So, what kind of headline works best?

One that promises the reader a large specific benefit. Personalize the headline by singling out the city, neighborhood, or group to which it is directed. Do not use humor – humorous headlines bomb 95% of the time.

- **Use size:** Our large pizza weighs 2 full pounds. Theirs is a puny 20 ounces – and costs you more!

- **Difference:** The difference between "premium" pizza – and "poor" pizza is this…

- **Newness:** Now – choose from 37 toppings, 4 sauces and thin, medium, or thick crust!

- **Use a question:** Who else wants gourmet pizza delivered in 30 minutes or less?

- **Too good to be true:** Is it immoral to indulge in pasta this delicious?

- **State it as a quote:** Would you believe it – our fajitas were voted "Best in town!"

- **Speed:** 90 seconds after you place your order – your pizza is in the oven!

- **Snob appeal:** For those few who will settle for nothing but the best.

- **Put a date in the headline:** August 12 –

- **Use a two-word headline:** $3 Breakfast!

- **Put the name of the city in the headline:** San Diego's Favorite Mexican Restaurant since 1939 – El Indio.

Quotation marks ("") increase recall of a headline by as much as 33%.

"Enjoy a Delicious Buffet Dinner with oodles of Variety – _only 9.99_ Per Person"

"Enjoy a _Romantic_ Dinner for Two in Our 'Couples Only' Section"

"Enjoy an Affordable, Delicious Lunch at Green Street and get a _free dessert or drink_ of your choice"

"Lunch Served _within 10 minutes_ From the Time You Order _or it's free._"

"Rusty Scupper Serves the Largest Selection of Seafood on the Waterfront"

"Free Wine With Every Dinner"

So, to wrap up here… people best remember the words at the beginning of a sentence (the primacy effect). And, the last words of a sentence (the recency effect).

Stack headlines so key words jump out.

Bold, <u>underline</u>, *italicize*, and use larger type to call attention to key words and phrases.

- Put the community in the headline: **Salt Lake's #1 Selling…**

- Put **YOU** in the headline.

- Put **NEW** in the headline.

- Put **FREE** in the headline.

- Put **Benefits** in the headline.

"Filet Mignon so Tender – it Melts in Your Mouth"

Instantly involves the reader by creating a vivid mental image

**If You've Already Gone Out to Dinner This Week,
Don't Read This – It Will Break Your Heart"**

Great lead in to a great dinner offer

"Prime Rib – *Without* the Prime Price"

Pulls the reader in with a promise of savings on a high perceived value dinner

"Who Else Wants Lobster for Only $14.95?"

Again, high perceived dinner – bargain price

**"Is it Immoral to Indulge in Chocolate Cake this Rich?"
"Only $1.99 with Any Dinner – This Week at Kona Grill"**

Add high perceived value to cake as break-even inducement to order dinner

Remember, a headline is the key to any ad. Direct marketers have proven this over and over. In fact here's an example from a direct mail test where a headline change added piles of cash to the campaign:

a. Auto insurance at lower rates if you are a careful driver

b. How to turn your careful driving into money

Headline "a" pulled 1,200% better than "b."

Do you understand what this means? If headline "a" pulled in $1,200,000... headline "b" pulled in $100,000.

And don't go getting crazy using hard to read fonts. Verdana, Arial and Tahoma have proven popular for web copy. The newspapers use Times Roman and Arial, or some variation of those. You won't see a bunch of different fonts in any newspaper. Do you know why? Eyeballs are fickle. The instant the eye lands on something "too busy" looking – it wants to go somewhere else.

This book is written in Palatino. Each letter has a little "foot" on the descender. This makes it easy for the eye to follow along a sentence without getting lost.

K ◄── That little foot is called a "serif." Another popular font is... **Arial** – Notice there are no little feet, or serifs. (Almost every coupon you see will be in an Arial bold type font.)

Headlines can be in Arial and the body copy in Times Roman. Or visa-versa. But don't use three or more fonts in the same letter or ad.

Or, **It** *gets* hard to *read*.

Always **Bold** your headline – and make it **Bigger** than the body copy.

And, It's Fine To Use Upper And Lower Case Like This On Your Headlines. It tends to add some oomph to them.

BUT, NEVER USE ALL CAPS – IT IS DIFFICULT TO READ.

It is okay to capitalize ONE or TWO words for emphasis.

Follow these rules and **YOUR** ads will **Sizzle!** Ignore them – and your ads will **Fizzle.**

Your headline has stopped them in their tracks. They're interested... now what?

Once you've flagged down your prospect with your headline, you've got to get them INTERESTED in your product. Remember earlier, how we need to make our headline call out to the right prospects – with just a quick glance?

If the body copy doesn't quickly pick up the pace with self-interest, and benefits, you will lose them. Much like a theatre would lose people if the marquee said: Star Wars, but the movie was Bambi. Star Wars brought them in. Star Wars is what they want to see.

Speaking of movies – remember, the job of your copy is to paint a vivid mental movie with your prospect right in the middle of it. They've got to "see" themselves taking the action you want them to take.

People never part with their money until they can clearly envision the benefits they will get from the product they buy.

Since the headline is already claiming a big benefit, we need to expand on that benefit. It'll be a bit confusing to the prospect to have a Status headline:

Announcing – The Most Delicious Gourmet Pizza, and Why You Should Try It.

And, then follow up with a bargain basement pitch like:

You'll immediately taste the difference between Randy's NEW Gourmet Pizza and "ordinary" run-of-the-mill pizza. Even though our ingredients are the best money can buy, our prices will surprise you.

In fact, you can get our top-of-the-line gourmet deluxe for the low, low price of only 9.99.

We were doing fine until we got to the price. The mistake here is flagging down the gourmet crowd and then going into a cheap price pitch. How can the best pizza sell at the lowest price? It can't. We've lost believability.

Now – You Can Enjoy Gourmet Pizza
<u>Without</u> the Gourmet Price – Here's How

You'll immediately taste the difference between Randy's NEW Gourmet Pizza and "ordinary" run-of-the-mill pizza. Though our ingredients are the best money can buy, our prices will surprise you.

In fact, you can get our top-of-the-line gourmet deluxe for the low, low price of only 9.99. How can we offer these incredible prices? We took the bold step of signing a 10-year contract with our food supplier. And, we've locked in the lowest prices – EVER!

Now – we pass the savings on to <u>YOU</u>!

Now I believe it. The headline works with the copy.

Finally—Great Tasting Gourmet Pizza
And – <u>90% Fat-FREE</u>!

After a headline like that, you're not going to start off talking about prices, or savings. You've flagged down people who want a great tasting – low fat pizza. Tell them why it's low fat. Tell them how and why it still tastes great.

Convince them with specific facts, or testimonials. Then make the offer. Then tell them how to order. Don't start with one kind of headline and then shift gears to another angle. If you start with low cost, keep rolling with low cost. If you start with taste, paint a vivid picture of great taste.

Such as: "The minute you bite into Randy's moist, succulent, tangy BBQ Chicken Pizza – your eyes will roll up. You'll let out a little sigh of pleasure. And, you'll just say, Mmmmmmm. I promise! <u>It's that good</u>!"

With Food the benefits are:

• **Taste** – Will it taste great? Prove it.

• **Savings** – Will I save money? How much?

• **Health** – Is it healthier than the others? How so?

• **Experience** – Will I have a great time? Explain.

• **Status** – Will my friends or neighbors be impressed? Why?

Most ads pass by sputtering and wheezing like so much buzz. A well thought out headline or opening grabs your prospect by the lapels, commands attention… and catapults them into a benefit-packed pitch that has them basking in the spotlight.

You'll find a comprehensive list of powerful headline words here: www.karingtongroup.com.

Balance of Power

Picture your prospect as having a perfectly level balance scale residing in their heads. Now a "balance" scale is exactly that. If one pan bears a load of 10 ounces, the scale can only be perfectly balanced when the other pan supports 10 ounces. In our mental scale, these pans are logic and emotion.

Your goal is to swiftly add weight to the emotional pan. Every now and then you'll also put a weight or two on the logical pan.

We're striving to outweigh any current associations your prospect currently has with any competitors.

You want this scale wildly out of balance with the emotional weight of your message, exceeding the logical weight by a decided factor. Once that happens, your prospect has "sold themselves." Once the emotional side of the scale has been loaded up, then you begin adding weight to the logical side. Tipping the scales of emotion creates the buying opportunity. Logic seals the deal.

Thought Control

An old song on the radio can launch a childhood memory, perhaps bringing sadness... perhaps a smile. The aroma of hot chocolate may transport you to a warm ski lodge. And a single word can pierce your soul, or send your spirit soaring.

It's as though our brains are riddled with trip-wires. And a passing melody, a pleasing aroma, or a sensitive word is all it takes to detonate an emotional explosion.

So, what exactly is emotion anyway? And how, exactly do you trigger it? I've puzzled over this throughout the years. I knew what I was trying to achieve, but I'd not seen a real "paint by numbers" formula in any of my marketing or advertising books (and my library extends into the garage).

Many words bring to mind a "picture." Think of: chair, carpet, tire. Pretty generic pictures – right? Now, think of: Rape, suicide, suffocate. How about; Triumph, miracle, pleasure? Words containing an emotional component invoke a "feeling." We'll refer to these as *power words*.

Legendary copywriter, John Carlton, describes power words as: "Any word that carries its own emotional wallop. Nobody reads a good power word without having their heart beat a little faster, their mind explode with old memories, or at least a tiny part of their system taking notice."

One of his examples is the word "humiliate." See how he uses that word in this headline:

How does an Out-of-Shape 55 Year-old Golfer Crippled By Arthritis & 71 Lbs. Overweight, Still <u>Consistently</u> Humiliate PGA Pros In Head-to-Head Matches By Hitting Every Tee Shot Further And Straighter Down The Fairway?"

Now, I remember getting the snot knocked out of me in 4th grade right in front of a girl I had a crush on. That was humiliating. I was so embarrassed, I didn't go to school for several days. This headline pulls from that experience, but it puts me in the dominant role because as long as I read the ad and order the product... I can *do* the humiliating, rather than be its victim. It could also have gone the other way: "PGA Pros Consistently Humiliated by..." So, the word – all by itself conjures up a "feeling" as it navigates my psychological terrain.

And it is feelings that create the desire to buy things. Logic allows scarce resources to be allocated to the acquisition because the decision is in balance. Of note, very wealthy people (no scarcity of resources) think nothing of dropping $382,000 for a Rolls Royce Phantom, despite the fact they are no more reliable than a Toyota. But guess what? That expensive pile of leather, rubber and metal "feels" wonderful. The fat price tag is part of the feel-good feeling too because the fact they can drive something most can't afford, makes them feel even better.

Not so fast though. I see ads every day that are loaded with "emotionally charged words" but fail to stir the emotions – even a little. Rookie writers having read a book or two, mistakenly assume that an artist is born by simply applying paint to canvas. Van Gogh studied his craft and spent years getting to understand perspective and color. So, yes... anyone "can" slap paint on a canvas. It's the rare person who can put that paint in a spot pleasing to the eye.

Okay, so we have words that create pictures in the minds-eye. We have words that trigger feelings. Then we have words that do neither, such as: Delicious, large, spectacular. Words invoking no "minds-eye" picture or failing to trigger an emotion need to be put into some context in order to have meaning. As an example: "Our Most Spectacular Hawaiian Vacation Sale Ever!"

What exactly does that mean? For me it could sound pretty exciting if I was booking my first vacation to Hawaii. "Wow, I better check this out." For you, it might bring back memories of a dank motel room three miles from the beach and a bout of food poisoning. "Ugh… I'll never fall for that again." So, rather than allowing each reader to apply their own individual interpretation… we'll use "message control."

"Spectacular 5-Star Hawaiian Vacation for the Same Price Others Spend for a Cheap Motel and Breakfast Vouchers"

"Do you remember the most magnificent vacation you ever had? Where you enjoyed luxurious surroundings, pampered service and 5-star meals? Well, your next vacation can be just like that at half the cost because of a computer glitch that under-booked our most sought-after ocean-front property…"

Now, the word "spectacular" might spark a twinge of emotion because of a spectacular sunset you recently shared with a loved one, but it's pretty vague. Digging deeper offers up a few more treasures that prove more appropriate. Such as: Romantic, exotic, or extravagant. Those words conjure up some deeper emotional associations.

Now remember, a primary reason many ads flop is because the advertiser has made the ad all about "them." You can't expect to open a door to your prospects' emotional riches while talking about yourself. The standard "company" focused ad forces a prospect to watch the company take center stage. Most in the audience immediately begin hunting for an exit.

Here's a great opening from Omaha Steaks that puts you smack-dab in the ad:

"Can you recall the best steak you ever tasted in your life? One that was tender, juicy and just full of flavor. I'll bet you can. Most likely, it was served at an exclusive restaurant or supper club." It goes on to talk about how you can impress your friends by serving these same "fork-tender" steaks at home. But see how it puts "you" in the ad? And how it starts to associate their steaks with a prior experience you've had?

Descriptive words, woven into little stories put the reader in a place where they can access their own emotional experiences. They become the star. And since it's about them... they become absorbed with the plot.

Let's take an emotionally-charged negative word: Suicide. "Is Your Business Committing Suicide?" That phrasing shifts the "punch" away from you, and onto a third party – your "business." But, what if you said: "Do You Have a Suicide Pact with Your Competitors?" That becomes personal. You feel it in your gut.

The word "love" for example. How can you use that? "You'll Really Love Our Pizza." That's about as lame as it gets. You're not opening a door to an emotional anchor; you're just throwing the door. However, what about building a message around a parents love for their children?

Try this...

> Red Rock Pizza likes to think that parents, who care, won't settle for just the cheapest pizza. They'll consider the value of fresh ingredients, the benefits of great taste, and the pleasure in giving their kids something satisfying. Red Rock Pizza also knows that kids may not care about such things as freshness and quality, but of course, that's what moms and dads are for. Parents can feel good about serving their family Red Rock Pizza. Kids'll love the taste – you'll love the quality and everyone's happy.

This creates theatre of the mind. It puts them in the role of a good, caring parent who would never jeopardize their children's well being by serving that nasty fast-food pizza. They can visualize their children enjoying a good, satisfying meal. It binds the *word* with an established *association*.

I wrote the following ad copy for a new pizza concept here in Las Vegas. My aim was to paint a picture of quality ingredients, which connects the dots to great taste without the empty "best pizza in town", boast that even the discount shops use.

> Somewhere between the brick ovens of Italy and the delivery cars of America, something went horribly wrong. Traditional pizza, made with homemade bread, rich, creamy cheese and hand-picked tomatoes, is now tricked out with inflated "fast-dough," skim-milk, water-added cheese, and sauce from factory-farmed tomatoes. Enough... is enough.
>
> We didn't set out to make the most expensive pizza, or the cheapest... but to bake a good honest pizza... hand-made from scratch, baked in an old-fashioned flame-fired oven, and to also guarantee each pizza to be delicious – or your money back.
>
> Here's what you can expect from Ciao, Ciao...
>
> **Dough:** Why do we age our pizza dough for several days? Because, like fine wine micro-brewed beer or premium cheese... flavor characteristics are obtained from the delicate interactions between yeast and sugar. This takes – time. The more time, the better the flavor (which is why fine wines, beers and cheeses cost more).
>
> Complex flavors, delicate character and subtle nuances are achieved during this aging process. Sure, it's more work. But, until you've had a pizza made from properly aged dough... you can't possibly know what you've been missing.
>
> **Sauce:** Yes, it's true. We do import tomatoes from Italy. Why? Because, unlike factory farmed, mass-produced tomatoes that are saturated to the exploding point with water to provide saleable "weight" – these tomatoes are grown (and prized) for one thing... "Extraordinary taste."
>
> Each tomato has a "moment" when nature imparts a sweet, satisfying – full-bodied taste. Our tomatoes are picked at that

moment – no matter the size. That is "why" we import "these" tomatoes from family farms in Italy.

Cheese: Instead of "skim" milk, water, and artificial fillers found in mass-produced fast-food pizza-cheese... we use a premium, rich whole-milk mozzarella... specially made for us from centuries-old techniques. It is the richest, most flavorful cheese you will ever taste on a pizza.

Bake: Obviously, with this much invested up front, we can't just drop your pizza in a conveyor oven and hope for the best. Your pizza will be fire-baked in an old-fashioned brick and stone-hearth oven. The intense heat pulled "up" from this stone gives the crust an amazingly golden crisp texture (that cannot be achieved by the quick "blasting" of a conveyor oven). This "proper" bake takes just a few extra minutes of careful tending... and I promise, you will taste the difference.

So, if you value fresh ingredients, the benefits of great taste, and the pleasure of treating yourself to a satisfying meal... then I invite you to join us at Ciao, Ciao...

Precise wording creates what we see and feel in our mind. Control the language and you control the images conjured up and the feelings felt.

Put your prospect in the ad, they are the star. Use anchors (we'll talk about those in just a bit) to guide them to the personal experience you want them to associate with. Apply power words as needed to trigger specific emotions. Paint a complete and vivid picture for your prospect.

Buying Triggers

Over the years, our sense of smell has shrunk, and is quite under-developed for an animal of our size. Even the visual processing area of our brain is smaller than in comparably sized animals. But the area of the brain that processes language – is enormous! It dwarfs all other creatures. Nations have been moved to war, and consumers have been moved to spend, by well-chosen words.

Harvard social psychologist, Ellen Langer, obtained some interesting results from an experiment using the word "because." Her experiment consisted of people waiting in line to use a library copy machine and then having experimenters ask to get ahead in line.

- The first excuse used was: "Excuse me, I have five pages. May I use the copy machine because I'm in a rush?"

This request coupled with a reason was successful 94% of the time.

- The second excuse was: "Excuse me, I have five pages. May I use the copy machine?"

This request was only granted 60% of the time. A significant drop.

Okay now the shocker.

- In the third experiment, the experimenter asks: "Excuse me, I have five pages. May I use the copy machine because I have to make some copies?"

Notice how silly the reason is. "I have to make some copies." Everybody standing in line needs to make some copies! With no reason mentioned, just the word "because," a full 93% of the people said yes simply due to the word "BECAUSE."

The word "because" caused 93 people out of 100 to let a stranger move to the front of the line. The word "because" was a "trigger."

> "Our pizza tastes better than theirs "because" we don't use frozen dough" – is much stronger, and more *believable* than – "our pizza tastes better than theirs."

Using the following psychological "trigger" words can massively increase your success.

The Only.

By starting any sentence with – The Only – you are claiming dominance. The ONLY restaurant with the (blank).

What about Size?

How many Quarter Pounders would McDonald's sell if they called it the "4 ouncer?" Would you rather have just a "pint" or, a "full half quart?"

Make sure your sandwiches have a **"Full Half Pound of Meat"** instead of 8 ounces. Make sure you use a **"Quarter Pound"** of seasonings in your sauce – instead of 4 ounces. Are your pizzas a **"Large 14 inches"** or, only 14 inches? If it's 16 inches – it's an **"Extra Large."**

Make size work for you – not against you. For example: "Two full ounces of pepperoni" doesn't sound like much. Even though we used "full" – we used it between two small sounding words – *two* and *ounces*. You'd be better off saying, "Loaded with pepperoni."

No Other.

Want to sound better than the competition on things they do just as well as you do them? No problem. No other burrito comes with more fillings than Randy's Burrito's.

They might come with just as much "filling" as yours, but it *sounds* like they don't. No other sauce contains more flavor and seasonings than Mario's marinara. No other bagel shop has a better customer satisfaction guarantee than Randy's Bagels.

Will?

Can you deliver in 32 minutes or, *Will* you deliver in 32 minutes? Saying you **WILL** do something, sounds stronger than saying you CAN do something. We will make your pizza – just how you like it and we will deliver it within 32 minutes. Sounds pretty definite to me.

Because.

The word "**Because**" will strengthen your selling position "because" it makes you explain why. We have the best selling steak in the area "**because**" we use Black Angus prime, aged beef. We deliver faster than anyone else "**because**" our mapping program shows the fastest route from our store to your home or office.

Limit.

When you place a limit on something it seems to make people want it more. Stores have found that saying "Limit – 3 per Shopper" almost guarantees everyone will buy three.

Maybe your "special" is so good – you have to say:

Extra Large Cheese Cakes great for Thanksgiving – Only 8.99 each. At this price – only 3 per family – please.

Placing limits on certain specially priced items might juice the sales. And, you can certainly have a little wiggle room if they want four.

When.

When is better than if. *When* you want really great "Chinese food" call…. Is less challenging than – *If* you want really great Chinese food call… When means *when* they decide – not *if* they decide. Also, saying "If" almost implies they don't have the common sense to get really good Chinese food.

As Soon As.

As Soon As – can be more potent than when. In the right situation. As Soon As you place your order. Is more immediate than *when* you place your order. As soon as – is right now!

(Many) Danger word.

People prefer Randy's Seafood because (blank). This is better than, Many people prefer Randy's Pizza because (blank). It's funny, but the word "many" sounds like "fewer."

1. Our ingredients are costlier than our competitors.

2. Many of our ingredients are costlier than our competitors.

The first one implies that all of your ingredients cost more. The second one implies that some or a few cost more. Many can sometimes sound like *less*. Watch out.

(In) Danger word.

"In" can be a weak word. The best *in* pizza. The word *in* does nothing to help here. You'd be better off with: The best pizza *because…*

Just.

Just makes it sound like something you *just* did. Right now. I *just* checked my records and realized that you haven't ordered for a while. So, I wanted to send you this postcard good for a FREE loaf of garlic bread with your next meal.

Doesn't' it sound better than: I checked my records and realized that you haven't ordered for a while. So, I wanted to send you this postcard good for a FREE loaf of garlic bread with your next meal. The word just adds a little zip.

Each.

"Each" sounds very personal. Each pizza is hand made to order. Is better than: All pizzas are made to order. The first example implies individual attention. The second one lumps them all together. Don't over do it by saying: *Each* and *every* pizza is hand made to order. You have just reduced the individuality of each by saying that every other one gets the same thing. Each is mine. *Every* – is *every*body else's. I just care about mine.

Read.

Reading is work. Looking at something is easy. Don't ask people to *read* your menu. Or, read on to see what others have to say. Ask them to take a look at your menu. Or, see what others have to say.

One.

Do you have *a* dish that really stands out? Or, do you have *one* dish that really stands out? Do you see how the word "one" points the finger right at – that *one*? This special will run a "week" doesn't sound as specific as: This special will run for "one" week.

More and More.

When you say: *More and more* people are switching to Randy's Pizza. It sounds as though a ripple effect is sweeping through the community.

I.

"I" is very specific because it represents YOU. *I* guarantee each pizza to taste great or your money back. This is stronger than: We guarantee each pizza to taste great or your money back. *I*, is the owner/manager. *We*, is the faceless company.

Even.

"We deliver – FREE!" is fine, but: "We *even* deliver – FREE!" is better. Makes it sound like nobody else does it. Gosh, they make this great pizza for me and they *even* deliver it free. Our pizza was great before – and now it's better! Our pizza was great before – and now it's *even* better! See how the first one makes no sense? And, the second one sounds like the pizza is *even* better than ever.

Select.

Do you *use* the finest ingredients in my meal? Or, do you: *Select* the finest ingredients for my meal. Select is fancier than use.

Complimentary.

The word "Free" has the stopping power of an elephant gun. But sometimes you want to appear more dignified. And, sometimes you just don't want the crowd the word FREE brings out. Just make it *complimentary*. They'll get the message.

Unlike Others.

Unlike others implies... others do something that you don't. "*Unlike others*, we don't use lard in our dough." Does anybody use lard in their dough? I don't know. Maybe. But, unlike others – you don't. *Unlike others*, we haven't raised our prices in over 7 years. It's good to be *unlike others*.

Ordinary.

More and more people prefer the taste of Randy's Pizza over *ordinary* pizza. Ouch! One quick stroke of your brush and wham! – You've painted a picture that your pizza is better than ordinary (everybody else's) pizza. Who wants ordinary?

Also, note the use of the word "over." I could have said "to." But, *over* conjures up images of victory. "Regular" can be used too. But, it is a little softer than ordinary, as you can see: More and more people prefer the taste of Randy's Pizza over *regular* pizza.

Even though "old fashioned" is sometimes used to denote "out of date" – old fashioned pizza sounds pretty tasty. So, don't call your competitors old fashioned unless the word truly works for you. For example: Why punish yourself with old fashioned inventory software when you can have a solution that runs itself?

Plus.

"Plus" is a stronger motivator than "and." You get a large combo pizza, and a large 1 topping pizza for just 17.99. Let's add some octane. You get a large combo pizza, **_PLUS_** a large 1 topping pizza for just 17.99. "Plus" amplifies the second item.

This Same.

Do you have the same pepperoni pizza that – say, Domino's has? 14 inches. 6 ounces of cheese. 2 ounces of pepperoni. Can you beat their price? Do you want to? Then you could say: *This same* pizza sells for $14.99 at Domino's. At Randy's Pizza – you pay only 10.99. Also note that we used a $ for them, and not us.

Is, and Has Become.

"Randy's Hamburger *is* the best selling hamburger in town." "Randy's Hamburger *has become* the best selling hamburger in town."

The first statement sounds like everybody already knows about Randy's great prices. The second statement sounds like more and more people are discovering Randy's great prices. In the first, you're the 900-pound gorilla. In the second, you're the come from behind underdog. Shades of gray, for sure. But each tells a slightly different story.

Okay.

- You've claimed the high ground by having *the only* pizza with this, that, or the other thing.

- You've made your pizzas bigger by having a *full half-pound* of cheese instead of 8 puny ounces.

- You've told people that *no other* pizza has what yours has.

- You've convinced people that you *will* do what you say.

- You've explained that your pizza is better than the competitions' *because* of the extra things you do.

- You've had to place a *limit* of 3 per family because of your crazy low prices.

- You've told where to come *when* – not "if" they want a really good Chinese.

- You've told people that *as soon as* they place their order – you'll spring into action for them.

- You've learned to steer clear of *many* and *in*.

- You've found that by *just* checking things out, you can reactivate Lazy customers.

- You've seen how paying attention to *each* pizza; makes *each* of your customers feel very special.

- You've learned that *reading* is work, and that *looking* at something is easy.

- You've seen that having *one* of anything makes it stand out.

- You've told how *more and more* people are discovering your great tasting pizza.

- You've built trust with people by saying "*I* guarantee each pizza that *I* make."

- You've told people that your pizza was good, but now it's *even* better.

- You've made extra effort to *select* the finest ingredients.

- You've offered *complimentary* items to the upper classes.

- You've made it clear that you are u*nlike others*.

- You've clearly explained why your pizza is far better than *ordinary* pizza.

- You've told them they can get a large combo *plus* a large 1 topping pizza for only **17.99**.

- You've also told how t*his same* special costs less at your place.

- And, you've explained just how your hamburger place *has become* so successful.

Anchors

Comparing something about your product to a commonly known *fact* creates an instant shortcut for your reader. Instead of allowing them to arrive at some erroneous preconceived notion – or worse yet, invent something in their mind that entirely misses the mark, control your message with an anchor.

> Here's an example: Why is our Dough so Crispy, and Chewy?
>
> Well, a lot of fast-food pizza places claim "dough made fresh daily." So what? Great tasting dough requires time to develop a "complex" taste. Like Micro-brewed beer, or fine wine, it takes time for the yeast to fully impart "character" to the dough.

Here, beer and wine are our anchors because everyone knows aging is required to develop great flavor. So, we avoid blathering on about the "why" by connecting it to the "known."

I chose a particular treadmill because the salesman was able to provide an anchor: First he told me it had the lowest impact rating. But think how empty that statement is. Compared to what? Then he said: "Running on this treadmill gives you less impact than running on grass." I instantly got my head around that.

I'm often faced with a newbie client who is adamant about chasing after new customers, with little concern about getting current customers coming in more often. They spend a lot of money on advertising, yet they don't know who shows up or how to inexpensively contact them again. This is a common rookie mistake.

I make the comparison that spending money to bring new customers through the front door, with no way to reach them again is "about as crazy as trying to fill up a bathtub without a stopper in the drain." Bingo! They can see all that hot water circling down the drain, and of course – immediately see the financial consequences to their own pocketbook.

But imagine if I just told them how wasteful it is to advertise without some type of follow-up customer marketing. Since they're not currently doing any, the concept is a bit fuzzy. The analogy or "anchor" brings it into sharp focus.

We know how stupid it is to waste hot water filling a stopper-less tub, so of course it's stupid to waste money chasing after new customers with no way to keep them.

Subliminal Control

Nancy, and I went on an amazing adventure... traveling completely around the world, visiting Tokyo, Beijing, Moscow, Amsterdam and Paris. Now, call me funny but... I rarely buy souvenirs while traveling. Just never have. While some people have display cases packed with trinkets from every journey... all I buy are few postcards because they look better than the snapshots I take. I'm just NOT a buyer. Or, so I thought...

Our tour guide in Beijing took us to a silk factory... I was practically yawning as we entered. But then the girl had us handle real silk cocoons... let me operate the machine that unwound over a mile of silk from a single boiled cocoon... and she even had us get "hands on" with making a silk comforter. Then it was off to the factory showroom... I loaded up on silk presents. They also gave us a small gift.

The next day we stopped by a factory where Chinese vases are made... we saw the intricate copper work being performed, the application of colored minerals, the kiln firing, the reapplication of color... and more firing. Then several polishing stones of varying coarseness to buff the vases to a spectacular shine. Then it was off to the factory showroom... we bought a vase. They gave us a gift.

Nancy was asked if she'd like to learn how to tell a real pearl from a fake. Why not? So we popped into a pearl factory. Our guide pulled a fresh water oyster out of a tank and just about had a knife in it before I intervened – telling her I didn't want the oyster's death on my conscience. So, it was straight upstairs to the… factory showroom of course. I managed to convince Nancy that the "small" pearl earrings looked better than the big expensive ones. And we were off to the Great Wall (with another little free gift).

The day before leaving, we sat down for a traditional Chinese tea ceremony. After tasting and learning about all the exotic varieties – I bought 5 tins of tea and a porcelain tea set (funny – I'm not a tea drinker). They also gave us a gift – a pee pee doll (you can imagine what it does when water is poured on it).

Lesson: They began each "tour" with a fascinating behind the scenes look at how the item is made. This is "educational marketing." Once you're fully mesmerized by the process… bam! Out to the showroom where you begin to explore. Of course… you're already "sold" so now it's just a matter of picking out the right item. After the purchase – a little gift.

They never bragged about the product or tried to sell me. Instead they demonstrated the painstaking care in which it was made. They established its rarity. They let me – sell myself. The after purchase gift made me feel I'd received more than my money's worth.

That's my personal experience from traveling the world. We can see another textbook example by traveling back in time to the early 1900s, when the Schlitz beer company was fifth in nationwide beer sales.

They called in advertising great – Claude Hopkins to see if he could give them a boost. Claude was the advertising genius of his day (making over $500,000 a year!). Many of the products in your home (Palmolive soap, Quaker Oats, Goodyear Tires) would not be there at all if not for Claude Hopkins.

Anyway, Claude hopped on a train and went to visit the Schlitz brewery. Once Hopkins arrived, he was shown the beer-making process. The Schlitz process was not unique, all the other beer companies made beer the same way. But, Claude Hopkins, like anyone who'd never seen the process, was amazed at seeing these details for the first time.

The water for the Schlitz plant came from 4,000-foot deep artesian wells, which guaranteed its purity. The yeast used in fermentation was the result of over 1,200 experiments. All the yeast used for making the beer came from that one "mother" yeast cell. Special wood-pulp filters removed all impurities from the brewed liquid. There were special rooms with filtered air so the beer could be cooled without impurities. Pumps and pipes were cleaned twice daily to avoid contamination. The glass beer bottles were even steam cleaned four times before being used.

Hopkins was fascinated by both the complexity and quality standards of the whole procedure. He asked the Schlitz executives why they didn't tell people about all these things they did to make their beer so pure. Schlitz executives replied that they didn't think it was important because every beer was made the same way.

Hopkins said, "Yes, but the others have never told this story," and went on to create an advertising campaign that explained every step Schlitz took to make their beer so pure. (I've included his "Perfection of 50 years" ad on the next page).

Every beer manufacturer essentially made beer the same way, but Schlitz was the first to explain the process of creating "pure" beer and, by doing so, claimed a "pre-emptive marketing advantage" over its competitors.

Guess what happened… Schlitz became the number one selling beer in the nation in less than six months. And remember – all beers were made the exact same way. But this was the first time anybody had told the story.

Perfection of 50 Years

Back of each glass of Schlitz Beer there is an experience of fifty years.

In 1848, in a hut, Joseph Schlitz began brewing. Not beer like Schlitz beer of today; but it was honest. It was the best beer an American had ever brewed.

This great brewery today has new methods. A half century has taught us perfection. But our principles are 50 years old; our aims are unaltered. Schlitz beer is still brewed, without regard to expense, according to the best that we know.

We send experts to Bohemia to select for us the best hops in the world.

An owner of the business selects the barley, and buys only the best that grows.

A partner in our concern supervises every stage of the brewing.

Cleanliness is not carried to greater extremes in any kitchen than here.

Purity is made imperative. All beer is cooled in plate glass rooms, in filtered air. Then the beer is filtered. Then it is sterilized, after being bottled and sealed.

We age beer for months in refrigerating rooms before it goes out. Otherwise Schlitz beer would cause biliousness, as common beer does.

Ask for beer, and you get the beer that best suits your dealer. He may care more for his profit than your health.

Ask for Schlitz, and you get the best beer that the world ever knew.

Ask for the brewery bottling.
J. L. STACK

Ads like this quickly propelled Schlitz past all competitors...

What Claude Hopkins did was simply take the everyday, mundane features of brewing beer, and tell the story of how those "features" translated in to great taste (the benefit).

The moral of the story: Be the first to educate your customers about what you do for them. And tell them "why." How does "what you do" benefit them?

With "show and sell" you're presenting a fascinating behind the scenes look at how your product is made. The time, and care and carefully selected components that go into the finished product. Never do you make a sales pitch. And while a prospect is in learning mode, their defenses are down. They are very receptive. They either come to appreciate your product or they don't. But at least their mind is wide open instead of shut tight like with most "we're the best" advertising.

So don't holler about the "best" pizza in town. Show them. Prove it. Your ads and menus should take customers behind the scenes… tell them about the fresh ingredients, the homemade sauce, the real garlic… let them sell themselves on your pizza. Then… give them more than they expected. A little gift…

Your pizza dough is pretty much the same as everyone else's (or is it?). It contains water, oil, flour, salt, yeast and sugar (maybe garlic powder or some other seasoning). And to you there's nothing very remarkable about it – so you run around hollering "Dough made fresh every day." (Yawn)…

But now let's put on our marketing cap, pre-empt the competition and lay claim to the finest, most delicious crust in town. It's really easy…

Our Crust is a labor of love

People often ask, "Why is our crust so delicious and crispy?"

Well, a lot of fast-food pizza places claim "dough made fresh daily." I wish it were that easy. But it's not. It takes 50 pounds of premium spring harvest flour, 27 pounds of specially filtered water, 20 ounces of 100% pure virgin olive oil, 8 ounces of Premium Hawaiian Gold raw sugar, salt and yeast, and then – 72 hours of careful aging to create the finest pizza crust in Columbus, Ohio.

Here's how we do it…

Flour: You can get cheap flour all day long. And many pizzerias buy flour based solely on price. Big mistake. Because low-grade flour will never make a great crust. Here's why. A very high protein content is required to bake a great crust. Inferior flour doesn't have the gluten needed to support the gases that cause the crust to rise during baking. Poor cell structure results in limp, (often soggy) pizza crust. We use high gluten "Spring Harvest" flour. And of course, being the best flour available means it costs more than substandard "budget-priced" flour.

Water: And let's not forget the water. Pizza dough contains about 30 percent water by weight. And while many others simply twist open the tap and let whatever's in the pipe flow out... we take great care to use pure, crystal clear – filtered water. There's no point in using high quality premium ingredients if you're just going to mix them with tap water. That's why we filter our water through a special reverse osmosis filtration system, removing chlorine, lead and other contaminants. It's the equivalent of using bottled water. And because of this extra step – you'll notice the difference between our crust and ordinary crust in just one bite.

Oil: You'll find very few pizzerias willing to use real 100% pure virgin olive oil in their dough because of the added cost (some actually use cheap lard). But olive oil (a big part of the healthy Mediterranean diet) has a taste and smoothness unlike any other. That's why we won't use anything else.

Sugar: Refined white sugar is just "sweet" and lacks much in the way of flavor. We use Premium Maui Gold sugar from Hawaii (also known as "raw" sugar). This naturally amber-colored Premium Maui Gold is made by the slow boiling of layer upon layer of high-colored sugar. Premium Maui Gold adds rich, robust flavor to our crust because it retains its natural molasses flavor (you'll see).

Time: Great tasting dough requires time to develop a "complex" taste. Like beer or even good wine – time is needed so the yeast can ferment and impart "character" to the dough. It's a symphony of delicate interaction between yeast and sugar that makes a great tasting crust. That's why we age our dough (called proofing) for at least 72 hours – so it can develop the wonderful complex flavor that makes it taste so fantastic.

And of course, the same care goes in to our sauces and toppings. This is why Angelina's Pizzas are guaranteed to be the finest you've ever had.

Notice how you're not even thinking about the price? What you're thinking is: "This sounds damn tasty, I better try one."

This brilliant ad, written by Roy Williams (the Wizard of Ads), uses theatre of the mind not to sell the watch, but the adventure.

"You are standing in the snow, five and one-half half miles above sea level, gazing at a horizon hundreds of miles away. It occurs to you that life here is very simple: *you live or you die*. No compromises, no whining, no second chances. This is a place constantly ravaged by wind and storm, where every ragged breath is an accomplishment. *You stand on the uppermost pinnacle of the earth*. This is the mountain they call Everest. Yesterday it was considered unbeatable. *But that was yesterday*. As Edmund Hillary surveyed the horizon from the peak of Mount Everest, he monitored the time on a wristwatch that had been specifically designed to withstand the fury of the world's most angry mountain. Rolex believed Sir Edmund would conquer the mountain, and especially for him they created the Rolex Explorer. In every life there is a Mount Everest to be conquered. *When you have conquered yours*, you'll find your Rolex waiting patiently for you to come and pick it up at Justice Jewelers. I'm Woody Justice and I've got a Rolex... for you."

The story crawls right into your mind because it is telling... not "selling." Imagine if Roy had screamed about a $15,000 Watch...

Passion Control

Desire is more easily channeled than created. Crawling into someone's head and igniting a desperate need for something they hadn't even known about two minutes earlier is nearly impossible. But, persuading them to choose you to satisfy an already smoldering desire is child's play. We do that by piling on benefits. And even reinforcing those benefits with additional benefits.

Desire is very personal. It revolves around an "end result..." a benefit in exchange for cash. The last thing you want is a boat. And you certainly don't enjoy the prospect of hauling it to the boat ramp and off-loading it. What you desire is... the wind blowing on your face, the salt air, and the freedom of the sea. The boat is a mere feature, making the fantasy a reality.

Benefits answer that question. Features don't. When you talk about features you are talking about yourself. And, you MUST talk about your prospect – with benefits. Let's first find out – exactly what are features?

A feature is the size of your product, how many minutes it takes to deliver it, what ingredients are in it, how many toppings are on it, etc. A benefit is the enjoyment your prospect is craving – that is derived from those features.

Filet Mignon for example is the most tender cut of beef – but not the most flavorful. On the other hand, Rib-eye is certainly very flavorful. So, the benefits of Filet are tenderness. The benefits of Rib-eye are succulent, unbeatable taste.

The easiest way to picture this is to understand that you don't want or "need" grass seed. What you want is a green lawn. Grass seed is a feature. The green lawn is the benefit. Stick with me on this, because this is a "make it or break it" for all of your ads. Always start with the BENEFIT (them) and then explain with the FEATURE.

You could say: "Our large pizza will satisfy the whole family." How so? What does that mean? Or: "Your whole family will be thrilled with Randy's Extra Large Pizza – it's a whopping 16" in diameter, a full 201 square inches of mouth watering flavor – and loaded with a pound and a half of toppings."

WOW! The second one sounds huge! I'm convinced – it'll satisfy my family's appetite. Sure, it's more copy – but it "speaks" to them first and then tells them why. And, really – what does the first sentence say? Nothing.

How do we convert features to benefits? It's easy. List your features, and then ask yourself "what does my customer get from this feature?"

Feature: Three different sizes.

Benefit: The perfect size pizza for just you, or the entire family. Getting the right size saves you money and there's no waste.

Feature: Fast Delivery.

Benefit: No more waiting forever. Dinner will be on the table faster than you can heat up a can of chili. You don't have to spend any money on gas rounding up dinner. You can sit back and watch your favorite TV show while dinner comes to you.

Feature: Delivered in our "electric hot bags."

Benefit: No more cold pizza. Arrives piping hot for the whole family.

Feature: Gourmet taste.

Benefit: You'll be the "talk of the town" when you serve Red Rock Pizza at your next party. Impress your guests with the same flavor you could only hope to find in the finest restaurants.

Feature: Two-for-one pricing.

Benefit: Feed the whole football team for less than one dollar per person and, with the money you save – treat them to ice cream!

See how features can quickly transform into benefits? See how benefits paint a picture for the prospect and answer the big question: "What's in it for me?"

Now, please remember – start with benefits, follow with features. The features are what make the benefit "believable." Benefits are "them." Features are "you."

Pile on the benefits, convince with the features. And, always put your strongest benefit first. Don't bury it in the middle. And, don't save it for last (they might not get that far if you do).

Once your headline has pulled them in, they immediately want to know "what's in it for me?" Benefits answer those questions. You can use bullets to make a power list of benefits. A very powerful technique. We'll cover bullets in a next. Don't start off with small talk. Start off with a BANG! And, end with a BANG! Get those benefits out there in plain sight. Nobody's going to dig around looking for them. Put'em out front.

Bullets

Bullets are a great way to connect a string of benefits. So, instead of going on and on with a long sentence – break it up into quick benefit-loaded visual gulps.

It doesn't matter what you're selling. Every prospect will have different benefits they want from your product. You can easily push several "Hot Buttons" with a string of bullets.

Bullets are in fact – **"mini headlines."**

And, people can't resist reading, or at least skimming them for ones that push their hot buttons. So, Instead of saying: "We have 44 toppings to choose from, regular or thin crust, and fast delivery."

Let's create some winning bullets:

- **Choose from 44 gourmet toppings…**

- **Weight watchers? Try our thin crust – half the carbs…**

- **Delivered piping hot to your home in LESS than 30 minutes…**

We just took a ho-hum sentence, and turned it into a fast paced series of "hot buttons."

Here's some more:

- **You'll be choosing from 37 toppings instead of 12…**

- **You'll be getting 100% pure olive oil in your pizza dough instead of lard…**

- **You'll be getting whole roasted garlic cloves instead of powder…**

The last three were "comparison" bullets. Plus, we plopped the most powerful word on the planet at the beginning of each one. Now, let's make a quick distinction. Never use bullets to list features, only. Just take a look at how uneventful these bullets are:

- **Huge conveyor oven!**

- **B-flute boxes!**

- **10-line phone system!**

- **Under NEW management! (Somebody shoot me)**

- **The BEST food in town!**

Each bullet, a meaningless feature. The last two are minor league for sure.

Bullets are "action packed" motivators that quickly list why your prospect should buy from you.

So, here's the deal. Take your best features, turn them into benefits. Then make a bulleted list of benefits.

- **Bullets pull the eye**
- **They quicken the pace**
- **They add excitement**

Blind bullets: We'll delve into the power of the "open loop" in just a bit. For now though, pay very close attention here, because "blind" or open loop bullets are – bar none – the most powerful motivating force you can use in almost any ad.

The idea here is to hint at a juicy benefit, without spilling the beans. The prospect will discover the secret once they buy the product or come to the store.

Here's a postcard I used to drive traffic to a website that promoted my Black Book marketing system. If you were a restaurant or pizzeria owner, you'd have difficulty getting to sleep without having your curiosity satisfied.

Here are a few open loop bullets you would find on the website:

- **How to "cloak" your ads so they enter the brain's emotional "buying" center – unchallenged.**

- **Four words that boost profits by as much as 24% – when taking an order. (This "tricks" the brain's ability to say no).**

- **How a simple phrase will "instantly" boost your average order by 24.8%. You can put this to work the same day you get my course. (That one technique earned me an extra $58,823.52 in one year!)**

Benefit lists make it very clear – exactly what the reader gets. And, since they only care about themselves – benefit lists are a lethal marketing weapon.

One and two syllable verbs that indicate movement give power, life and action to your writing.

Create – Open – **Turn** – Keep – **Build** – Find – **Unleash** – Explode – **Uncover** – Break – **Tear** – Punch – **Rivet** – Drop – **Kick** – Stir – **Strike** – Spread – **Dig** – Throw – **Come** – Go – **Do** – Pull – **Cut** – Push – **Shake**

Using these action words in your bullets keeps your prospect centered as the star of the ad. Verbs arouse the subconscious mind too. The seat of reaction and emotion. Benefits created with lots of verbs literally turn into subconscious commands for the reader. And, the subconscious mind acts on commands. It is compelled to do so, that's what it does.

Bulleted benefit lists are irresistible. By piling on benefit after benefit – they have an astounding effect on the reader. And, done correctly, can get readers so exited – they have to take action right now.

Blind or "open loop" bullets create maddening curiosity that must be satisfied. Your aim is to make them so compelling, the reader wouldn't stop reading to leave a burning house.

Proof

All righty… I don't want any trouble here… just put your hype down and back away slowly.

Any claim you make is met with nothing more than a skeptical sniff unless you immediately back up that claim with proof. How many times have you seen: "The best pizza in town… at the lowest prices?" First of all, it doesn't make any sense. You can't have the best *anything* at the lowest price. And secondly, that's what almost every single one of your competitors claim too.

If it's the best… says who? What proof will end the debate? Show me the research or study. Ironically, proof elements are surprisingly easy to come by. I'm amazed, hardly anyone uses them. A simple photograph, testimonial, newspaper clipping, even your own story about your product is all it takes to convince a prospect that you are worth checking out.

Specifics

Specifics are believable, generalities are not. Even though Ivory soap is 100% pure it was advertised as "99 and 44/100 pure." Honestly – what sounds more believable? For it to be 99 and 44/100 pure – somebody had to do some research – right?

So, as we keep adding to our tool kit, "specifics" is a tool we'll want to use often. It heightens "believability." I'm sure you've seen pizza ads claiming: "Dough Made Fresh Daily." Now, I don't know about you, but when everyone uses it – it becomes meaningless.

How about this: **"Our dough is mixed exactly 9 minutes and 17 seconds."** Now, that's specific. But, it's still a feature. So, we would put in a benefit. **"Our dough is mixed exactly 9 minutes and 17 seconds. Our customers tell us it's the tastiest crust they've ever had – anywhere."** Now, we're starting to get somewhere, plus – we've aroused curiosity.

How does this sound? "At 7:15 every morning, I begin making the dough for our famous crust. I use specially filtered water – at exactly 89 degrees. The yeast we use comes from a special strain – stolen from a bakery in Italy in the 1700's and smuggled into this country. (Hey, I didn't steal it!) After all the ingredients are added – I mix it for 9 minutes and 17 seconds with my 1956 Hobart mixer. (Yeah, 1956 is the year it was made). After mixing – it goes into the walk-in to "proof." I keep checking it. When it's just right – I form individual dough balls – one of them will be for your pizza."

"Is all this work a pain in the butt? Yeah. But, our customers absolutely "rave" about our crust – so, I don't want to let them down. Is it the best crust in town? I think it is. But, I know this for sure – it tastes better than that frozen "chain store" crust with the cardboard taste." Now, is that a wonderful story – or what? Does it tell people that your dough might just taste incredible? Absolutely.

While "Dough Made Fresh Daily" falls flat on its face – everybody claims to do the same. This little story makes you unique. It makes your dough story believable. And it does it by being SPECIFIC:

- **7:15 a.m.**
- **Filtered Water**
- **89 degrees**
- **Special Yeast**
- **9 minutes 17 seconds**
- **Old Mixer**

You've also added "our customers rave about it." That's somewhat claiming to be the "Best." But, it's not you doing the boasting – it's your customers.

And, in the last sentence – you've piled on the benefit of "great taste" *and* painted the chain stores with the "cardboard taste" brush. Specifics are great. They make your wonderful story believable. And, you do have a wonderful story to tell. Claude Hopkins rocketed Schlitz Beer into first place in just months using specifics.

Demonstrate

In the middle of the 1800s most buildings in New York City were no higher than four or five stories tall. Not because we couldn't build them taller but, because elevators at the time – were death traps and used only for hoisting freight.

Because of this – people took the stairs and weren't willing to climb much more than four or five flights. But finally, a man by the name of Elisha Otis invented what he called the "Safety Elevator." He knocked on doors, talked with architects and builders – yet couldn't "sell" a single safety elevator.

Then one day, an announcement caught his ear. The World's Fair was coming to New York City. Elisha Otis hatched his plan and waited patiently. On a bright sunny day at the 1853 World's Fair – before thousands of onlookers, Elisha Otis climbed a forty foot platform and stepped out onto a working model of his Safety Elevator. He explained to the hushed crowd below that upon his command – the cable responsible for raising and lowering the elevator would be severed by his assistants.

Silence fell over the crowd and Elisha Otis stepped to the front of the elevator for all to see. "Cut the cable" he yelled! An axe swung, the crowd gasped. And twenty thousand eyeballs remained frozen as the new "Safety Elevator" locked itself in place – and didn't budge an inch.

Instead of Elisha Otis plummeting to his death, New York City rose into the sky. In a single instant the world was liberated to build into the clouds. One simple demonstration accomplished what years of "telling" people could never do. Demonstration proof is powerful.

And remember the slogan "The slow ketchup." We recognize it as the slogan for Heinz ketchup because it's been hammered home in the company's advertising for years. Beyond that, consider how it communicates the brand's promise – and unique benefit – that Heinz ketchup pours more slowly because it's thicker, richer and tastier than its competitors. And remember the commercials? Heinz ketchup was compared to a rival brand by pouring each into a paper towel. The rival brand dripped through – Heinz did not.

And certainly you recall the Pepsi challenge. People typically believe their own eyes over what you "tell" them.

Use Photos

Recently while traversing the Newark airport – I saw one of the finest examples ever – of a pizza shop backing up its talk with proof. While standing in line at Famiglia Pizza something caught my eye. A small cylinder of water with one of those little bubble-blowing aerator thingamajigs you see in fish aquariums. What was that all about I wondered? So, I read the little sign perched on top. It told how the water used to make the pizza dough – was brought in from New York, insuring the crust would taste the same at every Famiglia Pizza. Wow! Trucking in water is a lot of effort – but who would even know without this little "prop?"

Then pictures next to the menu boards show "Mama Rosa" in the olive fields of Tuscany. Another photo shows the owners hand selecting tomatoes from the fields of central California. Another shows "Paul and John" at the dairy farms in Wisconsin. Yet, another wall is jam-packed with autographed photos from celebrities.

Bottom line? Instead of claiming "best pizza in town" like many do – they "convey" quality with photographic proof. Proof that they truck in the water. Proof that celebrities eat there. Proof that they select quality ingredients. Without a single empty boast, the photographs say it all.

I took these snapshots in the Newark airport.
They don't "tell" you. They "show" you.

Photographs showing the product in use generate more interest. So don't show an empty restaurant. Show a crowded restaurant with happy faces. Don't show a riding lawn mower. Show a man sipping coffee, surveying his beautiful yard with the lawn mower visible out in the background. Photographs should convey the end result. And never underestimate the immediate proof conveyed with *before* and *after* pictures.

Testimonials

In his explosive 1928 book "Propaganda" Edward Bernays said; "In making up its mind, its first impulse is usually to follow the example of a trusted leader. This is one of the most firmly established principles in mass psychology." People automatically "follow the crowd" or a perceived leader (celebrity).

Testimonials get fence sitters off the fence. People want some assurance that they are making the right choice, that they are not alone. Your headline pulled them in. Your Unique Selling Proposition impressed them. Your Specifics convinced them. Now, your testimonials will convey added proof that others also like your product. And if you have good press – use that too. Get testimonials from some of your good regular customers.

Have them write a short letter, and get permission to use it along with their name. Don't use initials. It looks like you made them up. Use their full name. Nothing looks phonier than – Greatest Pizza in the World. N.H. Who's N.H? Put a real name. Go ahead and "coach" the customer a little bit on what you're looking for. Make sure they mention...

- **Low prices – how low?**
- **Variety – how much?**
- **Fast delivery – how fast?**
- **Tasty – how tasty?**

Or, whatever things it is that will reinforce your USP. Also, we want our testimonials to be specific, too. Remember – specifics sell. When I seek testimonials from clients, I send them a form. I ask specific questions such as: "What frustrations were you having before becoming a client?" And "How has Repeat Returns helped your business." I want specifics… not blathering generalities.

Compare.

> "Randy's Pizza is GREAT!"
> – *Fred Smith, Any town.*

OR,

> "A friend told me about Randy's Pizza. I was hesitant at first but my friend was so insistent that you guys had terrific pizza. So, last Friday night I called for delivery. It seemed like, no sooner had I hung up from placing the order – that your driver was ringing my doorbell! The pizza really was great. Better than any of that fast-food stuff I used to get. Count me as a regular from now on!"
>
> – *Fred Smith, Any Town.*

The first one lays there with all fours in the air. The second one is very specific.

- **Friend**

- **Terrific Pizza**

- **Friday Night**

- **Delivery**

- **Better than Fast-Food Stuff**

A rock solid way to get the testimonial you want is by providing guests a quick form to fill out. Use leading questions such as; What frustrations were you experiencing before coming to us? How have we solved your problem? What do you like most about us? You can even dress the form up as a "questionnaire" or a "survey."

Just put a quick sentence at the bottom indicating that you may use the comments in your marketing.

I've even used testimonials from the managers and owners of other restaurants including Starbuck's, IHOP, and P.F. Chang's. That's pretty powerful when a so-called competitor will endorse you. Plus, you leverage their reputation and brand.

WHAT OTHERS ARE SAYING

"When a friend enthusiastically referred me to you - I ordered your pizza. Delivery was incredibly fast. The price was a bargain. And the taste - was out of this world! I'm hooked!"
Yvonne Smith - Manager - Starbucks Coffee, Village Center

"**Red Rock** has taken pizza to new heights. It's just unbelievable that pizza this good can show up at your house! Words can't describe it. It's in a category all by itself!"
Mike Freres - Manager - IHOP, Summerlin

"**Red Rock Pizza** blows everything else out of the water. You will not find a better tasting pizza. Delivery is *FAST* and the prices are fantastic. It's what I get for my family."
Jason White - Manager - P.F. Changs

It's hard to argue with the extra credibility gained from a real person... with a title of authority, at a business that is instantly recognized.

Or, use the **"Someone Famous Ate Here Testimonial."** The Rolling Stones had my pizza. So did the first President George Bush. You can bet I let everyone know about that (especially the Stones). So, instead of bragging about yourself – have someone else do it for you. Get some testimonials. Use them. Be specific.

Amazon.com, Best Buy, Ebay... you name it, and they post consumer reviews and ratings. They encourage consumers to post testimonial reviews about books, products and services for the exact same reason we've just discussed. It reassures fence-sitters and moves them to action.

Press

A favorable write up in the paper a magazine or a respected online source is gold for you. It's the next best thing to having an earthquake open the entrance to a long-hidden gold mine. But here's the thing… once a review is in print or online, it sits there waiting for eyeballs. And in the case of print… well, the shelf-life is about as long as unrefrigerated fish. You need to take whatever press you have and take it out to your prospects and wave it in their faces. Most reviews will have plenty of great quotes to use. But, even a mediocre review can be salvaged for "testimonial" use.

Let's say you had an "off" night and your review went like this:

> "We visited Randy's Pizza last Friday night, and while the variety of pizzas is impressive, the service was mediocre at best. After an hour, our pizza finally arrived. Despite the bad service, the taste was fabulous." Pull the good stuff, and leave the rest.

"The variety of pizzas is impressive. The taste was fabulous"
– Joe Blow – *Dallas Tribune*

Press provides a light-speed shortcut to believability. Take for example if during the course of conversation I were to tell you that: On the way to an MTV video shoot for a band I launched, that was riding high on a Billboard top-40 hit, I'd been arrested for felony discharge of silly-string. Would you believe me?

When silly isn't so funny

Kamron Karington, manager of the Sacramento-based band Cause & Effect, was arrested Tuesday in Los Angeles for discharging a can of Silly String from a moving vehicle. Seems Karington and the band were on their way to filming a music video for their upcoming single, "Another Minute," when Karington shot Silly String at a second car carrying band mates **Sean Rowley** and **Richard Sheperd.** But a breeze carried the substance adrift, and it landed on the windshield of the Los Angeles Police Department patrol car following behind. Instead of the usual misdemeanor, Karington was charged with a felony for "discharging a dangerous object from a moving motor vehicle." Karington was released after the president of SRC Records posted $5,000 bail, just in time to see the final moments of Cause & Effect's video shoot.

Believe me now?

Note: I traveled to Los Angeles for a hearing on April 28, 1992 – and charges were dismissed. The very next day Los Angeles exploded into chaos when the Rodney King verdict sparked a week of rioting, looting, and murder. I watched on TV from home in Sacramento.

You'll learn why you better start collecting reams of testimonials in the "Rage Control" chapter (that ought to be enough of a hint). Collecting testimonials is so important, *especially* today that it's a built-in component on my Repeat Returns marketing program.

Unsubstantiated hype is not a tide that lifts your boat as more and more of it rushes in. Quite the contrary, it swamps your prospect with skepticism and scuttles your message. If you've got a safety elevator, cut the cable. If you fed the Rolling Stones, hang a picture of them at the table they ate at. If you have press… give it sustained life by putting it on your website.

Morphine Marketing

I deal with addicts all the time. Discount junkies that break into a cold sweat at the thought of quitting. Bad marketing, like drug addiction has diminishing returns. You're not getting high anymore… you're just frying your brain. More and more – brings less and less. Pretty soon, it doesn't matter how much you do… nothing happens.

Take the crazy pizza business for example… lots of instant gratification junkies out there riding high on epic discounting binges, frying their profits.

Imagine you're a soldier who has just sustained a serious, life threatening battlefield injury. Two medics are nearby… one has a needle and thread. The other has morphine. The needle and thread will stop the bleeding. The morphine will deaden the pain. You can only summon one medic – which one will you call? If you want to die with a grin on your face – grab the morphine. If you want to survive – you'll choose the needle and thread.

Likewise in marketing. You have two roads to choose from... one is short and leads straight to a cliff, crowded with lemmings. The other is a little longer but leads straight to the bank.

Let's take the second road today. Lookey here... I have a map...

It all starts with a big concept – the audacity to compete on your product or service – instead of the price. Imagine that – yes, you'll actually "sell" your product instead of slashing your prices. In fact, you might even raise prices because the more "sold" a prospect is on your product... the less price conscious they become. Once you've made the mental shift to compete on your product – effective ads will practically write themselves.

Now let's get something straight. You can't just "sell" your product in an ad and expect to get the greatest return. You must still make an "offer" to reel in the most prospects possible. The distinction here is that instead of cutting the price – you'll add an incentive to sweeten the deal. This is "value-added" marketing.

Value added simply means giving something free (or super discounted) along with the purchase of the featured product. For example: I bought a Tempur-Pedic mattress. They gave me two free pillows. What they did not do, is lower the price of the mattress by a nickel. They instead "sold" me on the benefits of billions of foam cells that would support me as if I were floating on a cloud.

Okay, let's talk pizza.

Two kinds of customers. The bottom-feeders who are in a constant struggle to find the lowest price, and the others... those people who are just looking for a decent value and stay fairly loyal once they've found something they like. Here's the funny thing... only 33% of people consider themselves coupon-clipping bargain hunters. While 67% say they're simply looking for value and are willing to spend *more* to get it. So, just based on those numbers – it seems crazy that most pizzeria marketing is aimed at the smallest and least loyal segment of the population (big opening for you).

And what those "dollar off" ads are saying is: "My pizza isn't worth what I've priced it at." Furthermore, the math of discounting reveals a sinister race with ruin. For example: A pizzeria running a 20% profit margin pockets $3 profit on each $15 pizza sold. So here's a question for you... how much do you make when you put out a "$3 Off!" coupon? Answer – not much, if anything. Like pouring battery acid on your bank account.

But what about value-added marketing – doesn't that dig into profits as well? Yes. There is no free ride here. The difference is this though... instead of doing a $3 discount which comes straight out of your pocket – you can offer a $3 add-on item "free" with the order of a pizza. The add-on is perceived at full price – $3. But, it only costs you a dollar in food cost – leaving you $2 ahead.

Here's my suggestion... if you are going to rebuild your customer base with value added offers... start off with something aggressive like free wings with any large pizza. Then transition to free breadsticks and salad. Then just free breadsticks.

Anatomy of a non discount ad.

Benefit

Since we're not screaming about a low price... we need to feature a big benefit to pull prospects into the ad. Start off by telling them what *they* get.

**The juiciest, tastiest wings in all of Miami are yours
FREE with your next order**

Now, magnify this value-added offer by creating a high perceived value for your wings.

Sell the add-on

These are no ordinary wings. These are the fattest, juiciest wings you've ever wrapped your lips around. A full quarter pound smothered in our private recipe wing sauce. They normally sell for 7.99 – but they're yours free with your next large specialty pizza. I figure if I can get you to try'em, next time you'll buy'em. (Notice above how quarter pound sounds bigger than 4 ounces?)

Call to action

Delay is the death of a sale. "I'll get around to it," means – never. So you must create urgency with a time limit. Very simple: Limited time offer good till May 17.

Getting off heroin may not be easy, but I've never heard of anyone who regretted it.

Of further note... paying for anything is always perceived by the brain as an immediate loss. Picture yourself reaching for your wallet, pulling out some money and handing it to a cashier. Think about that experience. Okay, now picture being handed a gift all wrapped up in pretty paper with a big bow on it. Your brain thrills at the "immediate gain."

That's why people spend so much more money when paying by credit card. They perceive the immediate gain of what they just bought... but the loss is pushed into the future where it becomes disconnected from the moment.

So, instead of throwing away all your profit and attracting a temporary spike of junk traffic... charge full price for your pizza, attract the larger 67% of the population looking for value, and make a dollar on the deal. Much better strategy for you. Focus people on what they get (immediate gain)... not what they pay (immediate loss).

I doubled sales in my own pizzeria in less than 31 days using nothing but a letter offering a free salad, garlic bread and a two-liter with the purchase of a large pizza. In fact, it was well over a year and a half before I even designed an ad with a coupon.

Offer

Remember earlier when I said advertising is a lot like fire? The offers you put out to your marketplace control your destiny as a business owner. Here's why. In a recent phone call I suggested to a client that he should raise prices a bit. He swore there was no way he could do that. I asked "why?" He said he had cheap customers and they would never come back if he raised prices.

When I asked why he'd built his business on cheap, coupon-clipping, deal junkies... he seemed puzzled. "What do you mean?" He asked.

"You choose your customers by the advertising and offers you use." I said.

"Wow, I never thought about that."

It's not exactly rocket science is it? You put out birdseed; you're likely to attract birds. Discounts will most likely attract bargain hunters.

If discounting and being the low-cost provider is your business strategy, that's fine. If you're not set up for this though, you'll be pouring cyanide into your own well. Think about Wal-Mart. They've used two slogans to burn their message in. "Always low prices. Always" and "Save Money. Live Better." Their strategy is to always have low prices... not constantly discount their prices.

We'll talk about coupons, bundling, price-point offers and value-added offers now.

Coupons

The good news is you don't actually need to put a reduced price on a coupon. I used coupons regularly to promote a three-topping pizza at $12.99. The coupons were mass-mailed and were always profitable. Funny, my three-topping pizza had a menu price of $12.99. I tested $10.99 and $11.99 and found absolutely no noticeable difference in response rates.

This strategy won't work across the board. I did have one guy (in five years) notice the price on the coupon was the same as on the menu. I gave him free garlic bread and he left a happy camper. If you're delivering or sending a product by mail, test this. If people come to your store and see price tags on your merchandise, you'll want to pass on using full-price coupons.

Pay attention to the offers you wrap in a dashed border. And apply what you've learned to make each coupon a selling machine. Here are two examples:

If your large 1-topping pizza (menu price) is $9.99 or higher... then that means the wings are free. The coupon on the right gains enormous power by using the word "FREE."

The package deal on the right gains added octane by using the word "Plus" two times to amplify the offer.

Saying "$5.00 Off" – cheapens your product. Avoid steep discounts – they're not necessary. Instead use "price-point" offers. Harness the traffic-driving force of coupons without crushing your profits.

What causes people to cut coupons is almost a Pavlov's dog-effect. Just like a dog will salivate at the sound of a bell if it hears that bell before being fed, people grab scissors when they see dashed lines around things they might want to buy. By all means, use coupons. Discounts are optional.

Bundling

In-N-Out Burger offers bundled meals on their menu board. Of interest though, is the price. The #1 consisting of a hamburger, fries and a soda... costs exactly to the penny, what those items cost if purchased individually. They are simply making it easy for you to purchase a complete meal. No discount. I've seen this at KFC too.

Bundle products that enhance one another. And either offer a savings on the bundle, or not.

Price-point

Rather than discount a $15 pizza down to $9.99 – settle on a "price" and then find a pizza within 50 cents to a dollar of that price to use in the coupon. **Example:** Let's say you have a large 1-topping pizza on your menu and it's priced at $10.49. You also have a 3-topping priced at $13.49. You'll choose the $10.49 pizza to use in your "$9.99" offer.

People with a specific price-point in mind will zero in on the price that fits their budget, and most likely order the product that goes with the price.

Reason why

Offers that seem too good to be true raise suspicion. We wonder "what's wrong with it." And as we talked about open loops earlier, the too-good-to-be-true offer creates an open loop. We need to close the loop by offering a valid, believable "reason why."

• End of year tax sale

• End of month inventory clearance

• Fire sale

• Rain damage

• Scratch and dent

• New menu item

• Over stocked

• Anniversary sale

• Manager special

Take a look at the top of an ad I created for Aircraft Tool Supply. Notice the benefits and guarantee. But also notice the reason why they have dramatic deals and $5.00 off… it's their 30-year anniversary…

Simply saying "50% off" is less compelling than "End of year clearance sale… many items 50% off." Connecting a reason for the discount closes the loop, and doesn't train customers to expect and wait for ongoing discounts. It provides a reason to act now.

Power of "3"

It cleans! It scrubs! It sanitizes! Whatever the magic is… three benefits or freebies is a potent way to seal the deal. John Carlton advocates the three-benefit headline. And my own testing has shown it to be a run away winner. I can offer two free items with a purchase and do well. But, I'll tell you – when I had three freebies in the offer, it was lights out.

Value added

Imagine if you were buying a $15 pizza… and the order-taker said: "We're running a manager special tonight… you can get a second 1-topping pizza for just $6 more." Click. With savings like that, you have to pause and consider it.

Instead of whimpering about lost profits though, consider this; if you're operating at a 20% profit margin, the $15 pizza dropped $3 to the bottom line. The second pizza is pure profit other than food cost. Most likely – another $3 in profit. That doubles bankable profit on that transaction.

Crazy like a fox.

Make the Offer

Since we've "told or sold" we don't need to resort to steep discounting to make every sale. The prospect wants it… we just need to "tip" them over the edge. So, instead of a suicidal "$5.00 off," let's craft an offer that works for you *and* the prospect.

The people you can "build" your business with, want added value – not cheap pizza. I've found that adding free items with a high "perceived value" – not only pull very well, but attract people that will repurchase without coupons. Offers that add value to the customer's purchase are proven winners.

Instead of doing "Buy One Pizza Get One FREE" which digs deeply into your pocket… "Buy Two Pizzas – Get One FREE" is very compelling. Yet it's financially viable for you. You sell *two* pizzas at full price and give away a third that hits you for about $3.00 in food cost. Another proven value-added offer is a free salad and garlic bread with the purchase of any pizza. In either case the prospect sees $10 to $15 in added value instead of just a $3-$5 discount.

You choose your customers. And quick-fix methods of attracting them will, over time, suck the life out of you, and destroy your business. Mindless discounting and desperation offers – is a tempting trap to set, until you find it is "you" the trap has snared.

Connect the Dots

Eyeballs get cranky when confronted by long, unbroken blocks of text. In this book for example, I use indenting to break up the text and keep the page count from going through the roof. But when writing an ad… keep sentences to two or three lines. What about one word sentences, can they add drama and flair too?

Yes.

The use of dots… and dashes – helps to add movement to your message. Even commas, that seem out of place, (like the last two) – will help control the speed, and flow of your message.

Also, use connecting words to transition from one sentence to the next:

"So, you can see… But first… As a matter of fact… What's more… How can I offer this?… Naturally you'll want to… And… Plus… But surely… Notice… But here's the thing…" This will help add a relaxed, conversational tone.

If writing a sales letter, there's nothing like a few dots to guide the reader to the next sentence, or even the page, that's because they create an…

Open loop

Most books and movies consist of an "opening… middle… and end." The opening sets the stage for what's to come. The middle elaborates and of course this is where the "plot thickens." And the ending is where the dots are connected… and all loose ends are tied up.

The exception is the "cliffhanger." This is where completion and closure are left hanging… this of course is to induce you to buy the sequel… or catch the next installment. Think "Lord of the Rings." "Harry Potter." "Star Wars."

They wrap up "most" of the plot… but they leave a little question mark in your head that drives you berserk… until the next episode.

This "cliffhanger" is an amazingly effective marketing tactic because of a mysterious "flaw" in the human brain. It's called an open loop. And our brains hate them… we want and *need* closure.

You see it in action every day… take the news for example. Before going into the commercial break… the anchor will say something like: *"Seven people plunged to the pavement from a popular downtown tourist attraction today… and you'll never guess which famous movie star was arrested at the scene. Were there any survivors? We'll have full details after the break."*

You'll be glued to your couch… till after the break.

Another example is from the largest selling publication in America, the National Enquirer. They employ some of the highest paid writers in the world. Their job is to get you to "buy" the tabloid. And they are experts at getting them to fly off the shelf… in fact it's been said that more people read the Enquirer every week – than have ever read the entire Bible.

Again… it's the "cliffhanger" or open loop.

Headlines like: **Britney Baby Shocker…** Murder Mom Drama Queen… **Ashlee Simpson Tailspin…** Dr. Phil, Only 3 Years to Live!

See, none of these headlines… connects the dots. They leave you hanging. You need to buy the magazine to get closure. A great headline in the New York Post was "Headless Man in Topless Bar." Gotta buy that one for sure.

The person who first discovered this phenomenon was Soviet psychologist Bluma Zeigarnik. And this state of tension has come to be known as the "Zeigarnik Effect." Simply put – it's that uncomfortable tension that's created in the brain when a task or thought is uncompleted. A "cliffhanger… or open loop.

Think of it this way: How many times have you had a name "on the tip of your tongue" but just couldn't quite come up with it? Drives you nuts… and then three days later the name pops into your head while you're backing out of the driveway.

And, remember the Game Show… "Let's Make a Deal?" Close your eyes for a minute and you can picture a typical contestant squirming, jumping up and down and going out of their mind – waiting to see… what's behind door number 3. And we both know "why." Curiosity is one of the most powerful human motivators.

So, from now on… don't let the cat out of the bag. Instead, force the prospect to almost uncontrollably – grab the bag away from you and rip it open themselves!

The open loop… is drop-dead powerful when used for the *right reason* in marketing. And that – is to move a prospect to the next step.

What to Sell

There he sat… as expressionless as an iguana as I explained how an ad I would create for him – with a great headline… loaded with benefits, a really smokin' hot offer and a no-questions-asked, money-back guarantee… would sink like a dropped anchor… and how he would be pouring money away with the tap wide open. It was a bit awkward for sure.

The client had tasked me with finding a way to advertise a fish pizza – that just hadn't caught on. It was his "pet" pizza. He loved it. I thought it was okay… and customers had already been given free samples. Yet it just wouldn't budge.

He figured some fancy ad would surely get this pizza moving up the sales channel and turn it into a signature item. Let's get straight on something right now…

A deep-rooted fundamental marketing "fact" is that you will make lots of money by selling people what they *already* want to buy. And that you can go broke "on the quick" by plowing your ad budget into promoting fringe items with little interest.

Take for example grocery stores. They advertise top-selling items only. Stuff with wide appeal. Things with proven ability to drive traffic. Items that cast the widest net over the marketplace. Milk, meats, soft drinks. They don't promote mouse traps, toilet plungers or liverwurst. Only stuff that brings in big crowds of shoppers.

I mean, ask yourself... do you normally respond to ads for things that you have little interest in? Umm... no? Same thing for your own customers. They pretty much keep ordering or buying the same things... over and over and over. That means... you should keep advertising the SAME things... over and over and over. (I'm not talking about cutthroat discounting either – I'm talking about "selling" your product).

I often see pizzerias for example, advertise a "Large Cheese Pizza" at a low price-point because they're afraid of scaring prospects away with a higher-priced offer. Now that's fine if Cheese Pizzas are one of your top sellers... if they're not though... you are advertising something with little demand... and the low-price offer is costing you more than it's bringing in.

Even though my pizzeria was widely known for "gourmet," I found it best to advertise the Combo, BBQ chicken pizza, and I'd always throw a veggie pizza in the mix. Why? Because those pizzas made the phones ring off the hook. Now, I certainly listed my entire menu on most ads... but used photos and offers for my top-sellers.

You'll instantly improve your advertising results by following this path of least resistance. And that is by advertising what people already want to buy from you.

Here are three easy ways you can figure out exactly what you should be advertising to drive the most traffic with the least money spent.

• What are your current top three selling products?

• What has been a crowd favorite for a long time?

• What are your big competitors advertising?

Okay... the mere fact that your top-selling products are your "top-selling" products means people *want* to buy them. Your marketplace has already told you what to advertise. Promote what sells.

Contribution margin

Certainly, the natural inclination is to promote products with a high profit margin. I'm not going to argue that, but I want you to eyeball the other side of the coin. I'll borrow this example from my good friend, Big Dave Ostrander.

Say you have three dinner items on your menu: Steak, salmon and chicken. Food cost on steak is 50%. Salmon 40%. And Chicken 30%. So, looking at it that way you have 70% profit margin on chicken dinners, 60% on salmon and only 50% on the steak.

You have exactly 100 guests tonight, and they will order whatever you want them to. Which dinner will you sell them? Steak sells for $30, salmon $20, and chicken is $15.

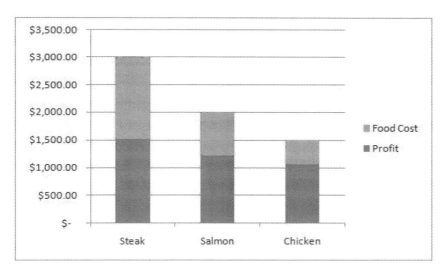

One hundred chicken dinners will give you $1,050 in gross profit. Salmon comes out to $1,200. And steak dinners yield you $1,500. So, oddly enough… the highest profit-margin dinner actually has the lowest overall profit.

Don't fixate on gross profit per item. Hop off the hamster-wheel, sell people what they want to buy, at a price that moves plenty of it.

Sell the Bargain... Not the Product

My crusade over the past several years has been to help pizzeria owners learn the skills to "sell" their product without slashing prices and relying on coupons. After all, two thirds of pizza buyers are simply looking to get their money's worth – and they're not necessarily looking for cheap pizza.

But... that leaves the other third that ARE looking for cheap pizza and low prices. So, how do you survive and even thrive in the midst of scissor-wielding coupon clippers?

If you find yourself surrounded by this persnickety pizza buyer, success will come from selling the "bargain" more than the product.

Selling the bargain begins long before we tackle the advertising. It begins with your cost structure.

1. Your biggest fixed cost is likely to be your monthly rent. If you're paying more than the grizzled pizza veteran down the block – (unless you have a far superior location) you're already in trouble. You either need a killer location with high visibility and easy parking – or a small space that gets the job done – and, on the cheap. A cruddy location *can* be used to your advantage in a price war. Tell bargain hungry prospects that you can sell so low because you have lower rent – and you are passing the savings along to them (they'll eat it up).

2. Food cost. Just because discount shoppers are more concerned about filling their gut – than emptying their wallet... doesn't mean they'll keep coming back for cheap slimy pizza. So, rather than hunting down the cheapest ingredients, it's vital that you nail down a prime vendor agreement with a supplier and negotiate the best price you can.

3. Portion control. There's been much said about this. Suffice it to say that McDonald's didn't get to be the biggest restaurant chain on the planet by letting each employee decide how much stuff to put on your burger.

4. Labor. Can't help you there. But I can offer a couple of hints that'll save you some cash. Cross-train all employees so they can perform any job. My drivers and cooks answered phones and took orders. My counter people could help out on the line and run an occasional delivery. Look at lunch sales… are you really making money or should you just open the shop at 4 o'clock?

5. Pricing. If discounting is your overall marketing strategy – then you can't start with rock bottom prices and then start cutting from there. You'll need to build the discount into the up-front price. $3 off a $5 pizza will surely get you into quick trouble. $3 off a $7.99 pizza – well, that's a different story.

If you don't have these numbers nailed down… you won't survive a suicidal price-slashing battle. Here are some proven tips for snagging the discount shopper…

First, let's understand what we're getting into when we chase after discount shoppers. They are not loyal. They will flit from bargain to bargain. Their only concern is getting as much as they can – for a rock-bottom price. They love coupons.

Now, I've made the analogy over the years that selling pizza is a lot like fishing. You'll reel in lots of fish by baiting your hook with their favorite morsels. People are no different. It matters not – what you the "owner" want to use to reel them in. It only matters that they the "prospect" are highly excited by. Let's begin.

Hooking the discount shopper without going to the poorhouse.

Tip: Prices ending in .99 are like heroin to a junkie. They scream – BARGAIN. Have all of your pizza prices end with a ."99."

Tip: An offer that reels in discount shoppers like moths to a flame is… *money off*. But if you just arbitrarily knock $3 to $5 bucks off the price of a pizza – you'll likely murder your bottom line. And, even though you don't see the big chains doing much of this anymore this tactic still hits a hot button with bargain hunters. But, let's not get carried away here. Grocery store testing determined (a long time ago) that the dashed coupon border generates more traffic than the discount."$2 off," without a coupon border generated *less* traffic than $1 off – with a coupon border. Try using "$1.00 Off" instead of higher amounts – and make sure you use a big, fat coupon border.

Other offers to test:

• Second Pizza for a penny (buy one pizza – get the 2nd for a penny)

• The more you buy – the more you save. First pizza is say $9.99, the next pizza is $7.99, and the third pizza is $5.99

• Take advantage of large pizza chain advertising… if they are doing a $5, $5, $5 promotion – piggyback by offering the same thing

• Buy one – get one half-price (at least you get your food-cost covered on the second pizza)

• Buy two – get one free

Tip: Use fonts that resemble the "sale" fonts you see on grocery store windows.

Tip: Put a slash through the old price and write the "new" price in next to it (with that grocery store font). Then, use that same font for all of your regular prices… it gives the "impression" that all prices have been cut.

Tip: Use bright colors (not too rich)… deep, rich colors look expensive and work against creating the perception of a bargain. People seeking cheap, cheap, cheap will be confused by a nice, rich look. It won't add up in their head. They'll be suspicious. Make the piece look the part. Like a three ring circus. Bright, primary colors – subconsciously reinforce your discount strategy.

Tip: Use the right media. Put inserts in the Penny Saver, Val-pak, Money-mailer… use flyers and door-hangers. Discount shoppers actively search for bargains – and go nuts when they come across these treasures.

Tip: Get your ads in front of bargain hungry prospects on the payday cycle.

You want to convey "Crazy, stupid prices..." without being crazy-stupid yourself.

Profit Control

A sea of over 400 faces looked back at me... it was 1:15 on Wednesday afternoon, March 21st. My "Pricing Secrets" seminar at Pizza Expo had just begun.

I asked a simple question... "how much does a can of corn cost at the store?" One person guessed... "79 cents?" Another – "a dollar twenty nine?" But nobody was willing to bet their life on the answer. Now, a short walk to a local grocery store would find someone who would... the store manager. He or she would in fact be able to tell you the prices of each brand, type and size of canned corn. They live with these products every day. They know them intimately.

So, this begs the question... what if I had a packed room full of moms and dads – your customers, and I asked... "how much does a pizza cost at the local pizzeria?" I'd venture to guess that I'd get a wide range of answers.

What does this tell us? Your customers have a vague idea of what a pizza should cost. But they don't have exact prices burned into their memories. On the other hand... you live with your prices every day and so – you do. Therefore, it's easy to make the false assumption that just because *you* know your prices like the back of your hand – that your customers do too. Not true. They're taking the kids to soccer games; they've got mortgages to pay and bosses to worry about. What you charge for a pizza – is the last thing on their mind.

As long as your prices are "in the ballpark" people will gladly pay them. And you'll gain a lot of pricing traction by "selling" your pizza instead of just pointing at the price with a discount. In fact – the important question you should be asking yourself is this… "Are my prices too low?" I'll bet the answer is – yes.

But, I have good news for you. Only 33% of people consider themselves "price shoppers" comparing prices on a regular basis. That means 67% are not price shoppers. They're simply looking to get their money's worth when they make a purchase.

Take a minute to internalize this… and ask yourself: Do you always buy the lowest priced products? Do you always compare prices every time you shop? Do you know the exact price of every item you have in your refrigerator? Do you ever run in to a convenience store and spend more for something to avoid the hassle of parking, finding an item, and standing in line to pay at a grocery store? Have you ever been concerned because something was priced too cheap? Do you ever treat yourself to a nice dinner at a fancy restaurant?

Okay, have I made my point? Good. Now, let me get out my pencil and whet your appetite with some whiz-bang math. Here goes: If your pizzeria is doing $200,000 a year with a 20% profit margin you'll pull in a $40,000 profit. An imperceptible 5% price increase – across the board will generate a 25% increase in pure profit – dropping $10,000 to your bottom line. This is free money with zero costs associated with it. Not even food cost.

How will customers react to your blatant grab for well deserved profits? When I raised my prices – I flat-out hiked every pizza by a dollar. And even though I'd braced myself for the shockwave – it never came. There was no whining by customers. No resistance… in fact – nobody ever said a word about it (made me want to do it again).

And then, I know some pizzeria owners who like to raise prices on a gradual basis… 5% here and there throughout the year. That's fine – I don't know that there's a right or wrong way to do it. I just know that you need to do it.

Here are some guidelines:

Lift prices that are stuck in the middle. If you have a pizza priced at $12.59, raise it to $12.99. If you have an $11.99 pizza – boost it to $12.99.

Add a dollar for…? Look for ways to add a charge for a premium topping or sauce. I had a pizza that for several years was priced the same whether you got it with marinara or pesto. Then one day I ran my food-cost on everything and realized that the pesto alone (to my complete horror) – cost $3.00 all by itself, to put on that pizza. On my next menu printing I put "add $1 for pesto."

Make sure you adjust the price of toppings too – so that a price hike does not conflict with a build your own price. True Story: I stood in my shop one evening while to my complete embarrassment – a woman pointed out to several customers that several of my pizzas could be purchased cheaper by building it from scratch – instead of ordering it from the specialty pizza menu. Ouch! Make certain that none of your "menu" pizzas can be built cheaper from the topping list. You don't want sharp-eyed mathematicians impressing their friends at your pizzeria.

Also, I'm not a big fan of discounting as a traffic driver – but let's talk about it for a minute. If your prices are too low to begin with *and* you're relying on discounting and "$3 dollar off" coupons to drive business… you're operating from a very vulnerable spot. However – raise prices $1 across the board (on pizzas) and those $3-off coupons are now only costing you $2 to redeem. Remember… people haven't memorized your pizza prices, they're just responding to the trigger "$3 off." Now, if you feel you have to discount to drive traffic – you're starting from a position of strength – not weakness.

If being the low-price, high-volume provider (like Wal-Mart) is your thing … great. That's a unique selling proposition or a strategy. It's not a temporary traffic-driving tactic. If you're not aiming to be the low-price provider then quit wobbling around in the kill zone. Raise your prices, "sell" your product – and don't blink.

Competitor Control

People often sputter and clutch their chest when I bring up the idea of guaranteeing the product or experience. Some faint. They're certain they'll be ripped off by boneheads and be catapulted to the poorhouse. And that kind of thinking is good for you… if you *don't* agree with it. That's because most business owners are petrified to offer a bold guarantee. The mere fact that you step forward and proudly flaunt your "complete satisfaction" guarantee… instantly separates you from competitors and opens up an eight-lane highway for eager buyers.

Again, ask yourself… if you were the customer, would you rather shop in a place that offers an iron-clad guarantee, or a place that says "all sales are final?"

Picture these two front doors:

1. This front door says: NO checks. NO refunds.

2. This one says: I Guarantee your complete satisfaction – 100%. Should you be disappointed for any reason – I will refund your money.

I feel better about door number two, don't you? So will your prospects. And, if you'll remember back – I talked about people buying with their emotions, but rationalizing with logic. Your ad stirs the emotions. Your guarantee goes a long way in satisfying their logical requirements. Today more than ever, people have been burned, taken advantage of, and down right screwed! They are skeptical. A strong guarantee will overcome that hurdle. Put the pieces of the puzzle together forming a vivid mental picture of the experience you intend to provide. Once that is clearly in their mind – make the big promise and close the sale with a bulletproof guarantee.

Domino's Pizza built a billion dollar empire on their 30-minute guarantee. Nordstrom's is famous for taking anything back. I mean, think about it… how many reputable retailers can you think of that don't offer a money-back guarantee?

A neighbor of mine owned a car lot in Salt Lake City. Over coffee one day, I suggested he use the following guarantee whenever a parent was shopping a car for their teenager:

During your first year of ownership, if this car should ever break down or fail to start within 150 miles of Salt Lake City, all your child needs to do is call this number: (_____). A tow truck will be immediately dispatched to return your child safely to your home, and bring the car to me. I will fix or replace the car within five business days to your satisfaction.

Gary loved the idea because he knew that only 2% of the cars he sold would ever have a problem within the first year. And think about it... if you were shopping for your kid's first car, would that guarantee help you sleep at night? It's a powerful example of mixing an emotional anchor to a powerful guarantee.

And check this out: I recently glimpsed a poster in Taco Bell. **"You'll Love It or We'll Eat It!"** Very powerful. If a fast-food place can hang a guarantee in their window, you can deploy a guarantee without worry.

I convinced a friend and Real Estate agent to adopt a money-back guarantee too. At the time, he was considering a change of career because of slowing sales. He was a tad hesitant, but figured "what have I got to lose?" and he ran with it. If you're unhappy with any aspect of the service he provides you, he'll credit you back his portion of the commission at closing. It's on his business cards and website. How many takers so far? Not one. And he started using the guarantee in 1999. Oh yeah, business has been booming too.

Remember, I had a strong, bulletproof guarantee and I only refunded 2/10ths of 1% of all orders that went out the front door. That's 2 out of a thousand orders. And guess what? We screwed up an average of 3% of all orders. Wrong toppings, wrong size, late delivery, etc. So, more than 90% of the people that should have asked for a refund didn't even bother.

Again, crawl into your prospects head. By the sounds of things... you've got about the most delicious pizza crust this side of the Food Channel. They like the offer – it's very compelling. The kicker is to make a big promise... something like: "If you don't agree that our pizza is the tastiest you've ever had – I'll give you your money back – every penny."

You don't even need to guarantee the product either. Guarantee something besides the *product*. You can offer a 20-minute take-out guarantee, or a 35-minute delivery guarantee, or "Every pizza has a full pound of cheese – guaranteed, or your money back." "Lunch on your table in five minutes or it's free."

A guarantee will generate far more business and customers than the infinitesimal amount of refunds you'll shell out by having one. So, ask yourself... do you want to generate 100 orders and two refunds, or 50 orders and no refunds?

Effective advertising gets beyond the "hunter and the hunted" advertising mentality. It looks long-term... to build a solid relationship. Sell your product. Add value. Guarantee the result.

Your strong, no-questions-asked guarantee helps people decide to act, and act now – today, immediately and without fear or concern. And, the more specifically you tell people what satisfaction looks like – the more compelled they'll be to order from you to receive the benefits you promise.

I used a guarantee in my Yellow page ad, and many of my clients have too (above). Of course the yellow pages are obsolete now... so put your guarantee on your website.

Always put the risk on yourself – never the customer. This makes it irresistible for them to purchase from you, because they have nothing to lose. This is a bold move most competitors fear to make. Seize the moment of decision with a worry-free proposition. Put your guarantee on everything.

A powerful guarantee devours any remaining doubt.

Take Away

The take-away can be a great way to bring a sale to closure. That's because it flips a switch in your prospects mind. It tells them flat-out, who should, and who should not buy the product. They can identify with one or the other. And it's a bit disarming too. Most ads scream that the product is perfect for everybody and will solve all of your needs.

However, when you point out "who should not order or buy the product" it requires the reader to decide which camp they're in.

For example… my Repeat Returns marketing program is a great fit for an already successful business, or at least a business run by a sharp owner. I really don't want bottom-feeders signing up for the program because it's not a silver bullet to save a sketchy business. So I pose this question:

Is Repeat Returns Right For You…?

Maybe – maybe not. Our program *will* increase sales in a financially viable – well run business, we see that every day *(and we guarantee it in writing)*.

It will not save a floundering business on the edge of bankruptcy.

- **If you're circling the drain, struggling to pay the bills…**

- **If you have issues preventing you from handling a significant sales increase…**

- **If you will not take action and enroll guests in the program…**

Then, this is not your answer, and you should pass. On the other hand, if you've got…

- **A financially sound business that you're looking to make even *more* profitable…**

- **A good reputable product or service, honest business ethics…**

- **And you will actively enroll guests in your program…**

Then Repeat Returns will take you where you want to go, and fast too – within the next 90 days...

Fact is, once the program is launched and you've enrolled guests – there's really nothing you can do to stop it from making you more money.

Listen to the difference Repeat Returns made for Tony Lippold... (There's a three minute testimonial from a client who got a $30,000 a month boost from our program).

So, I'm not claiming that my program will solve every problem you may have. I am saying that if you have a sound business and will enroll guests in the program, you should join. If you're on the verge of bankruptcy, you should pass.

While in the pizza business, my menus and ads stated: "We're not for everyone." I then explained how we use premium ingredients and that the cost may be a dollar or two higher than fast-food pizza.

Two things at play here. 1. I'm dividing people into two camps. Those who will spend a buck more for a lot more vs. the bargain hunters. 2. I'm bringing believability to the ad. The best does cost more. And I'm admitting my pizza is the most expensive in town. But I'm also quantifying that at a "dollar or two" more than the fast-food stuff. (By the way, serving my pizza became a bit of a status symbol in Salt Lake).

If you remember earlier – I said how it is "you" that chooses your customers? The take-away, helps you accomplish that with a certain degree of precision by forcing prospects to determine if they fit the buying criteria.

Call to Action

Without a close, or a call to action, an ad becomes a just a statement. Let's say you've done a decent job of creating interest and desire, and you have a good offer as well. Without a compelling reason to take action now, your ad becomes one of those "I'll get around to it" things. And, "I'll get around to it" – means never. Delay is the death of a sale.

A popular real estate course being sold on TV claimed that adding the words "get up and call now" pushed sales through the roof. Good salesmen know to close the sale and ask for the order. In the Million Dollar Letter I simply say; "Please – take us up on this offer tonight! But definitely before Nov. 25th." Due to the conversational tone of the letter, I keep the call to action low key, but reinforced with the November 25th deadline. Also, use a very specific deadline or expiration: "This offer expires Friday, August 17 at 3:30 pm."

So, starting today, every ad you write is going to:

• Grab their attention with a **HEADLINE.**

• Create immediate **INTEREST** with your offer.

• Follow with **BENEFITS.**

• Follow with **PROOF.** Testimonials, press, quotes, features.

• Make it **BELIEVABLE** with specifics.

• **GUARANTEE** their complete satisfaction.

• Use a **DEADLINE,** available for a limited time only!

• Call to **ACTION**, <u>call right now</u>!

Act now! Order now! Pick up the phone and call now! Good till August 17th. Command copy has the power to make the reader pick up the phone and order – now. Command copy creates an impulse to act.

Trojan Horse

Are you anxiously waiting to grab an ad and read it right now? Nope. Didn't think so. Neither are your prospects. Even the whizbang ad you spent three weeks creating is an unwelcome guest at best. Remember… the more your ad looks like an ad, the more your potential prospect will avoid it.

Personal Letters. The reason my Million Dollar Letter has proven so powerfully effective is because it flies under the radar. It is not perceived as an ad at all. It was more like a letter from a friend or neighbor. So, while the obvious junk mail piles up for later review (which usually means never)… my "letter" is being sliced open to satisfy curiosity.

Yes, it costs more to mail an individual letter than to piggyback with the other junk mail, but again, if your life depended on getting your ad looked at; you'd probably not trust it to luck. You'd want the highest probability of success.

For the highest open rate, have your mail shop use a handwriting font and blue ink for addressing. Use a real stamp instead of those printed "metered mail" indicias. You've already seen the jaw-dropping results this generated for me (it's done likewise for hundreds of my clients too).

Thank You Cards. Imagine for a moment… you've just stopped by a restaurant for the first time. The meal was good. The service was good. But, something unexpected happens. As the server brings your check to the table – you notice a man following. He waits just a second till the check has been presented – then he say's, "Hi, my name's Arthur Pedersen,, I'm the owner. I certainly hope everything was to your liking." With that said – he reaches in his shirt pocket and hands you a little envelope. He finishes up by saying "It's been our privilege to serve you today and I hope to see you again soon." He smiles and walks away.

You open the envelope and discover a hand written "thank you" card, signed by Art. It also offers a free appetizer next time you visit.

What has Art just done? Art has made a rock solid impression on you, that's what he's done. Art has made you feel special. Art has acknowledged you. Art said "thank you."

Plus, what Art has also done that you are completely unaware of is – he has slipped you a "stealth" bounce-back. Heck, you didn't even notice that till I just mentioned it. The bounce-back is disguised as a thank you card (free appetizer, remember?) Bang!

Do you know that most people never meet the owner of anything? Do you realize just how powerful it is to look them in the eye and say "I appreciate you stopping by?"

I have a friend who used to own the most successful nightclub in Salt Lake City. My friend Bob would walk the floor, stopping at tables and slapping someone on the back and saying "Hi man, it's good to see you again." And, he'd keep walking.

Now, the people at the table would ask, "Who was that?" "Oh, that's the owner; he's a friend of mine." Now, truth be told, Bob didn't really know hardly anybody's name, but he'd just call everybody "man."

Bob simply acknowledged people. And they love it. It makes them feel important.

I'll tell you a funny story about Bob. One night some goon slapped one of the waitresses. Bob hauled the guy outside, beat him senseless and threw him under a parked car. The next day someone calls and wants to talk to the owner. Bob takes the call. Well, it turns out to be this bozo from the night before. And he tells Bob that he got beat up at the club last night and is going to file a lawsuit. Bob says to him, "Oh, are you the guy they found the drugs on? The police are looking for you. What's your phone number?" The line went dead and the guy never called back.

Anyway, back to our stealth bounce-backs...

If you are the owner or manager, you have clout. You are top dog. Your acknowledgement is "gold." Do not underestimate the influence you wield. Now, people are doing business with you – not some faceless company.

Since I started teaching this technique in seminars, I've had people report stunning returns. One restaurant owner received back 84 out of 100 thank you cards – in 30 days. That's the highest return I've heard, but others are seeing 30%-45% all the time. And Michael Mrlik II, the president of Gatti's Pizza... attributes a recent 10% sales gain to that tactic alone.

Okay, here's how you do it: Go to OfficeMax or Office Depot and buy their little boxes of thank you cards. They're dirt cheap. Keep a specific pen handy for writing on these cards (always use blue ink).

Write out (or have someone with decent handwriting do it) something like this: "Thank you for stopping by. I really appreciate your business. And, please – use this card for a free (whatever makes sense) on your next visit." Then sign it.

Now, the reason I want you to use a specific pen for these cards is this... if you can get the customer's name – by all means, take out that pen and write their name on the top of the card, and on the envelope (don't forget to put a little comma after it).

Hand written thank you cards are "stealth" bounce-backs.

Free Report. Gary Bencivenga, copywriter extraordinaire, says to "make the ad itself valuable." Gary is famous for writing long-copy "reports." Now, the reports certainly contain valuable information, but the report's purpose is to position the person or product as the perfect solution to the problem.

Ads disguised as "reports" or white papers don't cause the defense mechanisms to spring up. Since they promise helpful information, we read with an open mind. By the time we get near the end, we'll start to notice an offer that entices us to try this amazing solution. And done well, the prospect sells themselves while eagerly devouring the helpful information in the report.

You most likely get these in your mailbox all the time. There are doctors who've discovered a cure for just about anything, or investment advisors that will triple your money in six months. Look them over. Notice how they make their pitch. You'll see catchy headlines, benefits galore, a money-back guarantee, and a compelling call to action. Learn from them. They're in your mailbox because they work.

You'll find a "report" I created for a financial company on my website: www.karingtongroup.com. There you can see how I positioned a tough-sell into an informative report that positions the company as the logical solution.

Grabbers. A grabber is something you insert – or attach to your mailing that forces the recipient to reach out and grab your offer, letter, postcard – whatever. Let's say you are mailing a letter to attract new customers.

Craft your letter. Headline (or, you can do without because the "grabber" gets their attention), offer, guarantee, call to action – but (here's the grabber part) staple a tiny bag of your "secret seasonings" to the top of the letter. Mmmmm? What for?

Because this will draw people in to the letter. First they'll notice there's something in the envelope because they can "feel" it. Then, when they actually see this mysterious bag one of the greatest motivators of all time kicks in… curiosity.

Yeah. They want to know what this little bag of seasonings is all about. So they start reading your letter. Here's your opening:

Dear Neighbor,

I know it's kind of goofy to attach a real packet of my Marinara sauce seasoning to this letter but I wanted to make a very important point. Look carefully at that packet right now.

Now, if you were to compare my seasonings to others, you would notice something alarming. Others put three times as much sugar in their sauce as I do. Why do some load their sauce up with sugar? To hook your children.

As you can see, my sauce is loaded with real "flavor" not just a bunch of sugar. Sure it costs just a little bit more but... what's an extra dollar when it comes to your family?

We slow simmer the onions, garlic and olive oil. Then we "fold" the seasonings in which "blooms" the flavor throughout the sauce. Plus, our sauce is blended from several different textures of tomatoes, and sauces. This gives it an amazing taste and hearty texture you just won't find with ordinary "runny" pizza sauce.

Yes, it's more work than just opening a can of tomato sauce and adding sugar like others do, but great flavor doesn't come straight out of a can.

Here's another approach...

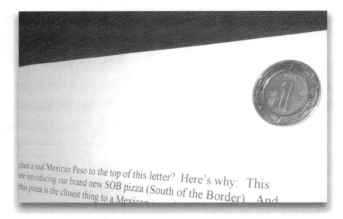

Embedded in the image:
> ...hed a real Mexican Peso to the top of this letter? Here's why: This
> are introducing our brand new SOB pizza (South of the Border). And
> this pizza is the closest thing to a Mexic...

*"Why have I attached a real Mexican Peso to the top of this letter?
Here's why..." then tell your story.*

Try using "grabbers" to boost response. You can even use grabbers in your business like Famiglia Pizza did with their bubbling tank of water. They stimulate interest.

When an envelope contains something more than just folded paper, open rates skyrocket.

I once began tossing what I thought was a piece of junk mail – into the trash. But something *caught* my fingers. Just a tad bit of bulk. There was *something* inside. Curiosity drove me to tear it open. Glad I did. It contained two tickets I'd ordered for a Rolling Stones concert in London. Whew...

The Two-step

Is it possible to sell a high-priced item with a postcard? No. It is easy though to arouse someone's interest and cause them to request more information. In direct mail, there's a correlation between price-point and the number of pages a sales letter needs to be.

A $200 gadget promising a better golf game may take just 3 or 4 pages of copy. A pitch for a $5,000 seminar can easily run 20 pages. A magazine ad will generate interest in a car; it won't take the place of a test drive.

So, rather than sending say, a 20 page letter selling a high-end seminar, you'd mail a small postcard to whittle down the audience to those most interested. Then you would follow up with the 20 page letter to those showing interest.

For example: I used postcards to drive traffic to a website to sell my Black Book. That proved more cost-effective than any other direct mail. You'll see that postcard in a bit. And pay attention to TV commercials and you'll observe a trend towards driving viewers to a website to get more information.

So, get clear before you pull up to the keyboard… *what is it exactly – that you want the viewer to do when they see your ad, TV spot, or email?* When creating an ad, ask yourself; "What's the goal?"

Do you want them to visit your website? A sales page? Call you? Simply reply?

Then write with the "end game" firmly in mind… don't go into a sales pitch in an email with some lame tag line like: "You can find out more on the website." Just write to get them to the website.

Also… and pay attention here… tell prospects "what to do" when they get to your website. You certainly wouldn't drop them off in the middle of a corn field and tell them to "look around."

For example: I will tell a new prospect going to our Repeat Returns website to…

1. Look at the amazing return on investment we're generating for others to get a feel for how much more money they can be hauling to the bank by joining our program (we show real-time ROI of current merchants on our program). If they like what they see there… then they should…

2. Watch the Webinar which explains the 6 ways we will increase their sales within 90 days…

3. Then I tell them to look at the "Repeat Returns" page… to see if our program is right for them…

I don't just say: "Go look at my website." So, look at your options and remember the two-step. A low-cost ad brings qualified prospects to the next step. And it could be a three-step. An ad on Google takes them to your website, where you have them opt-in to receive a "free" report or an in-home demonstration. Just remember to focus each step of the journey on the "next" desired action. Step one is written to get them to step two, which is written to get them to step three and so on.

You'll find, like I have… a small add, postcard or TV commercial will prove to be a great prospecting tool. You've seen the 30-minute infomercials on TV. They *can* sell in 30 minutes what would be impossible to sell in 30 seconds. So they don't even try to make a 30-second sales pitch.

Don't put too much, in too little.

Cash Control

Funny. Harvard just lost about $350 million in a hedge fund run by some hotshots with – of all things, Harvard MBAs. Seems like having a "Masters in Business Administration" from Harvard doesn't necessarily qualify the recipient as a "Master of the Universe."

Ironically the richest man in the world is a Harvard dropout. And a listing of the world's billionaires – is top-heavy with high school and college drop-outs. Hardly any MBAs. Again, funny.

What's going on here? Here's my take on it...

Precious few of us would be capable of surviving in the wilderness for more than a few days or maybe a week without some serious training. We'd be bug-bitten, starved, dehydrated, frail and near death. And while devouring a survival manual and keeping it clutched in your hands would tilt the odds greatly in your favor... the only way you'd be able to survive in the woods long-term is with real life experience. Trial and error. "Hmmmnnn... looked edible... but gave me a tummy ache. I'll avoid that berry from now on."

Experience rules.

And if you want to shortcut the learning curve... you better stick close to those who possess – real life experience. After all, do you want to wander into the woods with someone who's "read" about survival... or someone who *has* survived?

That brings me to the point of this whole thing. To make the leap from "learning" about something – to knowing it like the back of your hand – requires hands-on, real life experience. And what real experience gives you is the ability to fail small, and succeed BIG.

This is called *"testing."* Because others can "tell" you what has, or has not worked in their business... or what's blown up in their faces... or what's filled their nightly deposit bag with cash to the bursting point. But these guideposts are only a "point" in the right direction. For you... it could be the fastest path to a palm tree and a Margarita, or a blind alley. The only way to find out is by testing. Always test small before you roll out BIG.

And for sure, it's really dumb to create advertising by committee, and then take an all-or-nothing gamble on it. Better to roll out two or three tests at the same time. Different headline, different offer, different guarantee. And then if need-be, test these variables on different lists of prospects. That way, you'll have concrete answers instead of conjecture. Once you have proof in your hands, roll out the winner and then search for ways to improve on it.

Your marketplace will never lie to you. They will always respond to the headlines that catch their attention, the offers that motivate them, and the guarantees that comfort them.

Lavish them with value and respect, and they will open their wallets and favor you with their hard earned money.

Growth Control

Clop, clop, clop. The year is 1927. The dawn of a cool spring morning finds my grandfather delivering milk from a horse-drawn wagon in Salt Lake City, Utah. He and my great-uncle own a small dairy and delivery business. Today, my grandfather is delivering two routes, his and Al's, his brother in law. Al, having come down with a serious medical condition is unable to work. Luckily, each route has become a deep-seated routine for the horses. So, after delivering his own route, he returns to the dairy and hitches up Al's horse to the small wagon. Al's horse knows each stop on Al's route, by heart.

My grandfather is a bit put off however; when the wagon slows and then stops at a local house of "ill repute." But, what the heck… he figures the ladies have a right to drink milk too, so he heads up the sidewalk. Funny thing though… there's no milk box on the porch, so he knocks on the door. The Madam informs my grandfather that they don't take milk delivery, followed up with; "Where's the regular driver?"

Morning after morning… the horse stops, and morning after morning, Grandpa flicks the reins and pushes on to the next home. After a week or so… the horse passes right by the house in question, without even slowing down. My great uncle also had a little "habit." Unfortunately for Al, his little habit (the reason the horse was stopping) preceded the discovery of antibiotics.

To be sure, this family story underscores the power of a habit. Habits circumvent thinking. And habits are formed by repetition.

Habits are our mind's way of not having to rethink everything. Imagine if you had to start from scratch every time you needed to drive home. Fact is, half the time you pull into the driveway, you don't even remember the drive. It's an auto-pilot habit.

Habits are also, hard to break. Getting a new prospect in for the first visit is most challenging. Keeping them coming back is relatively easy. The words you need to know are: Reach and frequency.

In order to become an automatic part of someone's decision making process, you'll need to repeatedly persuade them to choose you with a frequency that is in sync with your products buying cycle. Example: Pizza is purchased more frequently than lawn furniture. So a pizzeria may need a frequency of 30 messages a year. An outdoor furniture store might get by with five or six during spring and summer.

Children are good at repetition. In fact, the average kid has to nag a parent nine times to turn a "no" into a "yes"… and they know it. In business, salesmen have to call on prospects, perhaps 5-7 times or more to make the first sale. And, they have to follow up after the sale to keep the customer's loyalty and trust. It's the same thing with us. I've had clients tell me "Oh, I've already mailed to everyone in the area." I'll say; "How many times?" Their reply; "Once." Putting a dent in the human brain is a process – not a one-time event.

Take Coke, Nike, and Toyota for example. Why do they keep advertising? They have some of the most recognized brands on the planet. Imagine if they stopped? Your business is no different. If you stop going after new prospects, your competitors certainly will.

So, gaining even a vague awareness in the marketplace comes from dogged persistence. Occasional marketing blasts produce occasional sales spikes… but not the momentum you need to move the needle permanently off zero. That comes over time with "reach and frequency." And the trick is – don't take on more geography than your budget will handle. A common mistake is… an owner trying to get too much marketing… from too *little* money. You'll gain much better traction by narrowing your reach… and increasing the frequency. So rather than mail 20,000 addresses every two months… mail 5,000 addresses four times in two months. Then move on to the next 5,000 and so on. That way, you make a series of impressions that build up, instead of a single pop that's easily forgotten.

People buy, when they're ready to buy… not necessarily when you're ready to sell. Now it would certainly make our lives easier if prospects and customers were sitting around waiting for us to snap our fingers. But they're kind of funny about that. They insist on getting what they want… when *they* want it.

So, if you're in front of them when they need your product, you have a chance at the sale. If you're not there, you're toast. If your budget can handle a big reach with the required repetition and frequency, great. If not, then drive traffic with a narrower reach, but more frequency. Capture customer data when they make a purchase. Use an automated marketing system to maintain a relationship with them. Then go after the next group. Consider getting your message out around paydays when prospects are flush with cash.

And as we discussed earlier, the mind seeks immediate gain while dreading immediate loss. That presents a deadly quandary for some. Many business owners cut back on marketing for an immediate gain. They're short on rent or payroll and since marketing is perceived as discretionary… they eliminate it temporarily to cover the immediate bills.

But, just like a moving freight train… even if you turn the engine completely off, it hurtles along for a while on its own momentum. That creates a "disconnect" as the owner sees no immediate, significant loss of sales. Then later on, when sales do start to slow down, the slump is not easily reconnected to the distant pullback in marketing. The two events are disconnected in time. Never forget that a reduction in marketing today will lead to a decline in sales tomorrow.

It's often a thin line that separates a serious marketing campaign from complete buffoonery. You're better off *owning* a smaller slice of your trade area, than none at all.

Don't spend too little... on too much.

Mr. Olympia

Las Vegas, September 30, 2006, in front of a screaming, packed arena – Jay Cutler is crowned "Mr. Olympia" – the same title once held by Arnold Schwarzenegger. Over the next few weeks, electrified audiences watch in stunned disbelief as Jay continues his unstoppable reign, sweeping across Europe winning even more titles. His face is plastered on muscle magazines, and million-dollar endorsement deals are pouring in. He is without a doubt the undisputed body-building champion of the world.

Fast forward to October 21... a massive Jay Cutler graciously greets me at the front door of his home. I've been invited to a celebration party his wife Kerry has (almost) surprised him with. "Mr. Olympia" happened to be my next door neighbor. This is not about body building though. It's about how the same principles that took a scrawny teenager from a Massachusetts farm – to the international spotlight... can be woven into the magic carpet ride – of your choice.

In case you couldn't tell... that's me on the left.

Muscle building requires eating like a horse, working out like a madman and sleeping like a baby (to recover). Jay eats portioned meals of mostly fish, rice, protein powders and certain carbohydrates at specific times throughout the day and night (he even ships his food to destinations when traveling). He works out 3 to 5 times a day – and sleeps in shifts. He does what most others won't. But, it's not complicated – in fact very simple. Monotonously simple. The real secret here is – doing the exact same thing that produces the desired result... over and over and over.

Same thing with sales building. It's simple stuff that most owners seem to tire of for some reason. They grow weary of their ads, offers and marketing long before their customers do. Now, there is a valid reason for that... "Owners" are acutely aware of this stuff – on a daily basis. Many have a distorted opinion that each time they put out an ad or offer, the entire marketplace drops everything and studies the ad.

This just isn't reality. Customers are not waiting like attention-starved puppies for your ad to show up. They remember your last ad (if they even noticed it) about as well as you remember the commercials you saw on TV last night. You should keep running the same ads, over and over and over – as long as they are driving traffic and making money.

Through centuries of puzzling and pondering, the holy grail of marketing has rested quietly in plain sight. By appealing to your prospects needs, wants, and desires, there is no need to hunt them down and twist their arms. Instead, they'll be attracted by massive benefits, and an indulging experience. Learn to give people what they want at a fair price and you'll go through competition like a hot knife through butter.

Allow Customers to Spend More Money

"The difference between the right word, and the almost right word –
is the difference between lightning and a lightning bug."– Mark Twain

I f your life depended on increasing your average sale… permanently, and starting tomorrow, what would you do? How would you
restructure the process at the moment of decision, the point of sale?

Strategy: With every transaction there is an opportunity for each
customer to gain more advantage or benefit for themselves. For just a
little more money, they can gain a lot more value.

In this section:

• See how and when to offer up-sells.

• Help customers choose by invoking the "herd" mentality.

• Why an exact phrase or "selling sentence" outperforms just "wing-
ing it."

• Learn how much more money a customer will eagerly spend each
time.

• Discover a way to have customers searching their minds – hunting
for more things to buy from you.

Never will you suggest or steer them into an additional purchase or
add-on that does not clearly and obviously tip the scales of value,
sharply in their favor.

Selling Sentences

It's true. 127,500,000 million gallons of water "leak" right through Hoover Dam every year. That's enough to fill 8,395 swimming pools. This water seeps unnoticed, silently, invisibly, through 7 million tons of concrete. Yet, this gusher is invisible to the naked eye. Your business also has a leak.

It's leaking cash, and lots of it. I'm going to show you how to harvest the hidden cash that doesn't appear on any balance sheet...that not even the best trained accountants could ever find. Every business has it, even yours.

Where is this mountain of money hiding? Right there in your customers' wallets – and they are eager to spend it. They just need a little help. And, you're going to provide that help through precise, proven, scientific means. Complicated? Not at all.

Up-selling is the easiest way to generate more cash in your business because it is practically effortless. It's done after the customer has already decided to buy from you. The truth is, it is a clinical and statistically proven fact that 30 to 67 percent of all people can be up-sold at the time of purchase. Of those, ticket increases of 15 to 25 percent are commonplace. They have already picked you. Their money is on the table. They are in "buying mode."

But many people either offend customers by being too pushy, or leave money on the table that customers would have willingly spent. Both options are costly.

How will up-selling affect my bottom line? That's a fair question. For savvy owners it will beef up profits tremendously. Let's say your ongoing net profit margin after all expenses is 10%. On each $10 purchase you make $1 in take-home profit. Well, what is your mark up? Do you mark things up 50%? Using that as an example: If you were to sell a $5 item for just $3 – *along with* the purchase of a $10 item, you would not be losing $2.50 in gross profit. You'd be adding fifty cents in net profit to that transaction. A 50% increase.

Take Starbuck's for example. I pay about two bucks for a large coffee, but if I want a refill, it's only about fifty cents. At that price I'll get one. At another two bucks, I'd probably pass. Once the original item is sitting on the counter, anything else purchased adds blockbuster profits. You will get rich by providing your customers compelling reasons to spend more money with you on each transaction.

But, as in everything, there are ways to shortcut the journey.

You Don't Say?

A test conducted decades ago by Elmer Wheeler, showed that a person faced with a choice of two different brands of shoe polish, and not sure which one to buy – could be influenced by just five words.

The salesman would point to one brand and say: **"This one won't rub off."** And even though neither one would rub off – the buyer would instantly pick the "won't rub off" over the other one.

(Did you catch what just happened?) As in the Persuasion Equation we saw earlier, a "problem" was introduced – and solved in just four words. A mental movie starring the customer flashed on the screen. The customer looked down and was annoyed to discover shoe polish on his trousers.

Here are a few examples from Elmer's book "Tested Sentences That Sell."

"Is your oil at proper driving level *today*?" Texaco got a full 50% of their customers to have their oil checked with this sentence. Maximum results were seen when the trigger word *today* was added. See how that specific word creates doubt? Gosh, I'm not certain if my oil is at the proper driving level – today... I better have it checked.

"It's our biggest seller." This of course brings the herd mentality into play. People want to go where others have already been. So this brings social proof to the purchase. If everyone else is getting this one – it must be the best.

"The family *economical* size?" This suggests a larger size that costs less per ounce than the smaller size.

Notice too, that in each case the selling sentence was used to benefit the customer. I'm grateful the service station attendant checked my oil and helped me keep my car in tip-top shape. I'm comforted, knowing this product is the biggest seller... that information makes my decision easier. And yes... it does make sense to buy the larger one. Even though it costs more now, it will save me money in the long run, making it the smart choice.

Now the beauty of these selling sentences is that you can take the guesswork out of up-selling. You'll find that some work well and some work very well.

Buy a pair of shoes at Foot Locker and they'll ask if you want a can of shoe cleaner. Buy a stereo and they'll hit you up for an extended warranty. Most restaurants push high profit drinks and desserts.

One thing's for sure. If you say, "Is that all" or "Will that be everything," you will most definitely throw cold water on the customer's buying spree.

Before you start licking your chops though, remember, we're here to help the customer have a better experience and enjoy doing business with us. So, up-selling is not about shaking the customer down for more money. It's about presenting options that may make the experience more enjoyable, or save them money.

Aggressively and robotically working the customer just to grab an extra dollar or two – will backfire.

A client of mine who owns a "national brand" chain of sandwich shops started an aggressive up-selling program. They were so successful, so skilled at up-selling – that customers who walked in expecting to pay about $7 for a sandwich – were ending up with $11 to $12 tabs by the time they got to the cash register.

This led to complaints. But it does point out how easy and effortless up-selling can be. I'll tell you exactly how much you can up-sell without causing any problems in just a minute but first I'll share an "aggressive" up-selling story from my own business.

I had a guy working for me. We'll call him "Doug." Doug would spend a little over two minutes on average, per phone order. I used to marvel at his selling ability. He would really work it. I'd hear him say, "Are you sure you don't want some extra cheese on that?" "Are you sure you don't want to make that a large?" "Can I get you an order of wings with that?" "Are you sure?" I assumed (for awhile anyway) that Doug's ticket average must be pretty high. After all, he cajoled, sold, and arm-twisted every phone call.

Then one month I held an "up-selling" contest. I was testing some "selling sentences." And all order takers were to work the extra cheeses, wings, and up-sizing. The winner got dinner for two at P.F.Chang's.

After one full month, I ran a server report on my POS and the results were tabulated. Doug was at the bottom of the list! The winner was a 16-year-old girl who simply followed instructions, and used the "Selling Sentences" that I was developing.

It seems that all of Doug's arm-twisting just turned people off. I mean, think about it. "Are you sure you don't want (Blank)." Yes, I am pretty SURE I don't want it! In fact, it's now very clear. When you keep asking someone if they don't want something – guess what? They don't want any thing else either.

The minute you come across as a pushy telemarketer, or used car salesman – your customer is going to quickly end the call. People are wary of being "sold." The minute a person perceives that they are being sold to – they put up the defenses. We're going to go right around those defenses by avoiding the words that raise the caution flag in your customer's mind.

Extra cheese on that?

On one particular night I asked 42 people if they wanted extra cheese. 26 said yes. That's 61% by the way! So, imagine – never asking! How much money is slipping away every day if you don't ask? A bunch! The beauty of up-selling sentences is that they are not pushy, and they flow naturally in the conversation.

Here's the exact technique: The customer calls and says: I'd like to order a pizza with pepperoni, mushrooms, and green peppers. Right there is *the time* to say: **"Extra Cheese on That?"**

If you were to say: "Do you want extra cheese on that." You cause the customer to stop and make a decision. This "interrupts" their buying sequence. And their thought process will be… "Do I want extra cheese?" "What will it cost me?" " Is it worth it?" A confused mind always says NO. Here are a few more examples to jog your mind…

- **Sandwiches: "Extra cheese/meat/veggies on that?"**
- **Steak: "Mushrooms and bleu cheese crumbles on that?"**
- **Bagels: "Extra cream cheese?" (People like "extra" stuff)**

It is simply a matter of finding the item that makes the most sense with the entrée. Then slip it in without asking a "question." Speaking of slipping, let's slip behind the curtain of the human mind and take a look-see as to why one way of up-selling out pulls the standard way by huge margins.

Since the buying process has a beginning and an end, the more effective and "unnoticed" your up-selling will be.

When someone is buying – they are in somewhat of a trance. They are focused on the buying experience. And they will stay in that trance until the purchase is completed.

Question; Do you remember a time when you were making a statement to someone or giving a talk – and someone interrupted you? And all of a sudden – you can't even remember what you were talking about?

That's happened to all of us at one time or another. When your train of thought gets interrupted – you are left searching for an elusive ghost that seems just out of reach.

The minute you ask a question by saying "do you want," you flip the customer from buying mode (right hemisphere) – over to the left hemisphere to process the incoming question.

It's the equivalent of throwing ice water on them while they're buying. There is one specific instance where you can ask a "question" and get an instant up-sell. And this one's a doozy.

This fabulous up sell sentence works extremely well if you know the order is for two or more people. Three variations:

- **"Would you like to share an order of wings with that?"**
- **"Care to share an order of Hot Garlic Bread with that?"**
- **"Like to share an Ice Cold 2-liter of Coke with that?"**

If they're dining in: **"Would you like to share an order of Hot Garlic Bread while you're waiting for your pizza?"** The key word here is SHARE. We all like to share something with someone we love. And, the word SHARE makes the mind visualize (very important) having a pleasant experience with someone we care about. **"Share" is a powerful "trigger" word.**

When a customer needs to choose between two or more options, you can help them decide by invoking the rule of "herd" mentality. People typically feel instantly more comfortable choosing what most others choose.

"Most people prefer the (Blank) – it's really good."

People like to take the safe route. When somebody is trying to decide between two items and asks you: "Which is better, the Garden Salad or the Caesar Salad?"

Simply say: **"Most people order the Caesar Salad – it's really good."** Three things are at play here. Crowd mentality, profit margin, and confirmation. We'll start with profit margin.

1. You make more money on the Caesar salad than the garden. If your Caesar salad has great flavor – your customer will be very happy with it and appreciate the recommendation. This will increase downstream revenue for you.

2. By starting off saying **"Most People Prefer..."** you are implying that the vast majority of people get that item. People like to follow the crowd. After all, if everybody else is getting it – it MUST be good.

3. By ending your selling sentence with **"It's Really Good..."** You are confirming that this is a good choice.

Also, when a customer calls and says "What are your specials tonight?" NEVER, start at your lowest priced deal. If you have a 9.99, a 12.99, and a 15.99 – start at 15.99 and let the customer work down from there. If you blurt out "we have a 1-topping for 9.99" right off the bat, you'll sell a ton of them. But, you won't sell many of the higher priced specials.

Start "higher" – let the customer lead you down to their comfort level. Use the word **"Plus"** instead of "and." What sounds better? "You get a large supreme and a large 1-topping pizza." Or, "You get a large supreme PLUS a large 1-topping pizza." **Plus** – sounds like you're getting something extra.

"I can make that a large for only..." or, "I can make that a triple pepperoni for only $2 more." This is a derivative of the McDonald's "super-size" up-sell. It's a great up-sell for those low-ticket one topping orders. No matter what they order, offer to make it "triple" for only $2 more. A variation of this is to offer to make it a 3-topping for only $2 dollars more.

When someone orders the basic meal – offer to "add-on" an additional item or side dish at a discounted price. And instead of looking at this as "discounting," look at it as adding profit dollars to your bottom line. Profit you would not otherwise be getting.

Occasionally, you'll run out of something. The best way to handle that is to say: **"WE JUST SOLD OUT OF (blank)."** Do you see the difference between sold out and ran out? If you run-out of something, you're not very organized. If you sell-out of something – you're very busy. Let's appear to be busy – not unorganized.

And at the conclusion of any purchase, just before you take the money and finalize the sale, you should say: "What else can I get for you?" Bang! Those seven words cause them to rack their brain to see if there is anything else they want. After you say: "What else can I get for you?" Pause briefly – then offer suggestions such as: "wings, cheese bread, (share?) etc.

Now, most of the time – they will be done – but – on occasion you'll find them blurting out something like: "Oh, do you guys have any root beer?"

The reason being – is that, again – you are staying "in step" with their buying process. Phrases like: "will that be all" – end that process. "What else can I get for you?" – stays "in step" with them.

And I will never, ever, ever forget the moron in the clothing store. Here goes… I walk in looking for a couple of shirts. When I come out of the dressing room, this idiot has pulled together a couple of suits, shoes and belts that "will go great with these shirts." Are you kidding me? I'm looking to buy two shirts for about $80 – and he's trying to up-sell me into $500 – $700 worth of suits. I dropped the shirts like a used hanky, gave him a funny look and headed straight for the door.

People will spend on average, 20% more than they anticipated. So if a customer is buying a $100 item, they'll readily spend another $20 on something that makes sense with the purchase. The chances of moving them to a $50 add-on are remote at best. Stick with this 20% comfort zone.

If your up-selling looks like a cash-grab, then you are clearly not looking out for the customer, and it will be glaringly obvious – thus defeating everything we've talked about so far. So don't up-sell and jack the ticket price just to make an extra buck. You want the guest to have a good time and not feel like they got fleeced. If an add-on makes sense – offer it. Don't instruct your people to pile on the pressure just to move the ticket up.

Add-ons or Cross-sell

This is a different animal altogether. You're not up-selling per say, or super-sizing the order. With an add-on, you're suggesting an additional item that enhances the enjoyment of the purchase. You might suggest a two-liter of soda with a pizza. You might suggest a complimentary set of tableware as a customer is picking out a dish set.

Amazon.com has this down to a science. If you buy mostly mystery thrillers, they'll always suggest other books of the variety you enjoy. And it's not pushy at all. In fact, I appreciate these suggestions and I've discovered many new authors this way. And when I bought my Kindle, of course, there were several covers to choose from.

Package Deal

A staple of fast-food restaurants, the "package deal" is perfect for most businesses. Take the typical car wash. You can get a basic wash, or a package deal that includes detailing, vacuum and tire treatment. They simply make it easy for you to spend more money and gain more satisfaction.

Amazon.com has mastered the package deal in a unique way. Most books sell for less than $25. However, you can get free shipping on orders of $25 or more. Might as well order another book right now (one that I'd get later anyway) and get free shipping.

People like to buy. It's fun for them. They are in control. The minute a person perceives that they are being sold to, their defenses spring up. By offering exceptional value with each transaction, you make it easy for people to choose you.

Keep in mind, up-selling and value-added propositions must always and obviously give the customer *more* value. It must always provide *more* enjoyment at a *lower* cost for them. The scales must always tip in *their* favor. Like moths to a flame, burn them – even once – and they'll vanish like smoke.

Enjoy More Customer Visits

"Half of my advertising money is wasted; the trouble is I don't know which half." – John Wannamaker

As it turns out, this often repeated phrase is wildly optimistic. Many small business owners find themselves chewed up and destroyed before they grasp the elusive secret… Mass advertising regularly squanders 99% of a precious ad budget without batting an eye. A steady diet of "spray and pray" marketing eats rookie business owners, alive.

The advertising and offers needed to gain *new* customers are not the same as those needed to keep them. Most struggling business owners keep pounding out the same cutthroat offers month after month, year after year.

They're disconnected from reality when it comes to equating spurts of junk traffic, with operating a successful enterprise. They have no method for targeting current customers, and in most cases – couldn't produce a customer list if they had to. They blunder and keep blasting shotgun marketing in every direction, hoping to hit something. Snipers don't use shotguns.

If your life depended on customers choosing you automatically without even considering competitors, what would you do? How would you build a fortress around them, making them feel appreciated, safe and comfortable with each purchase?

Strategy: Humanize your business so that customers are doing business with "you," and not a faceless corporation. Build a relationship of trust, friendship and respect.

In this section:

- Things are moving too quickly now. Don't kid yourself. If you already have the skills, great. If not find someone who does.

- The fall of mass-marketing is a gift. What once favored large companies, has become a millstone around their necks.

- Social media has leveled the field. The inside track belongs to the small business owner who moves quickly and decisively.

- Warning: Bad news travels at light-speed now, and can haunt you for years.

- Make the switch from desperation advertising to appreciation marketing.

- Would you give me a nickel if I gave you a dollar? Of course you would. Find out how you can build and lock in an amazing river of cash – for pennies.

- Take personal responsibility. Our minds can only develop solutions when we take ownership of what went wrong. Leaders don't pass the buck.

Do you have great service, low prices, the best "whatever" in town? Customers should just keep returning as though glued to a conveyor belt… right?

Being inebriated by the winds of over confidence will prove as dangerous as Magellan's misguided adventure on Mactan Island. You better start finding ways to show your appreciation to customers, and keep them loyal. And you'll want to get started on this right away… as though your life depended on it.

The Peter Principle

Entrepreneurs build. Managers manage. And marketers market. Three completely different skill sets to be sure. Yet a majority of business owners seem hell-bent on wearing all three caps. Surely, they'll save a small fortune by not "wasting" money on professionals. After all, how tough could brain surgery be? But statistics bear out a chilling reality... most new businesses fail – with restaurants high on the list of the "dearly departed."

I was talking with a client the other day and an old book I'd read almost 30 years ago came up "The Peter Principle" by Laurence J. Peter. The book makes a compelling case that people are promoted to their level of incompetence... that over time, success in one job or task is rewarded by promotions and more and more responsibility.

It goes like this... Bob does a great job working the front counter and taking orders. His smile could melt an iceberg. Customers love him. So, you figure... hey, if he does this good over the phone, just imagine if Bob were a delivery driver. Customers will just love Bob's great big smile and friendly chatter at their front door. Bob likes the idea of making more money and agrees to start driving.

After a while, you are so impressed with Bob that you decide to make him store manager. Bob is flattered and takes over the reins and begins his new adventure as store manager.

Makes sense. Bob did such a great job in his previous positions... that it only seemed fair to keep rewarding him with advances in position and pay. Only problem is... Bob's a lousy manager. You have unwittingly promoted him beyond his skill set. Bob's a great guy – but is now at his level of incompetence. And now, you're both in a pickle. You can fire Bob or let him run your store into the gutter.

That's the "Peter Principle" in a nutshell.

Now let's take this a step further. Is it possible that many good businesses falter and tank because well-intentioned owners insist upon doing tasks that they have little ability to perform? That they promote themselves into positions they have little experience with? The fire in the belly that drives many to open a business quickly subsides once the day-to-day running of the business settles into a dull routine. This is a great time to start hunting for a manager… or at least someone that's really good at what you are not.

From personal experience I know my strength as an entrepreneur is in marketing. When I bought my pizza shop, my own version of the "Peter Principle" quickly kicked in. Shifts went unscheduled, food went unordered, dough went unmade. Attempting to run the store *and* do the marketing was like doing jumping-jacks in quicksand. It was embarrassing.

So, as much as I'd like to think I can do it all… it's clear that I can't. I needed a *real* manager. Should I promote from within? Maybe. I mean, after all – they actually know this business better than I do. How hard could it be to schedule, order food, do inventory, see that prep gets done, equipment stays fixed? This should be a cake-walk with their young agile minds. Then something funny happened…

I remembered the "Peter Principle." Now, this was probably triggered by the cow-stupid stare coming from my dope-smoking cook, or possibly the hair-twirling, gum-chewing counter girl (her face looked like a test lab for eye shadow). It was clear in an instant that promotion from within was not in the cards.

Two states away, in another business altogether, was a lady I knew to be a "manager." She had cut her teeth in the family's 7-Eleven store as a teenager. Then she had gone on to franchise support. She understood the nuts and bolts of scheduling, ordering, customer service. All the details that keep a 7-Eleven humming along 24/7. In fact, the largest real estate developer in California had hired her away from 7-Eleven to baby-sit his 20 million dollar private jet, making sure it was always pretty, fueled up, and stocked with munchies.

And, I'm thinking… where do I find someone like that? I know – I'll call her! After all, wouldn't managing a pizzeria be a whole lot more fun than taking care of some stupid jet? After begging, groveling and lying through my teeth about the pizzeria being almost on "auto-pilot," Kimberly Streeter agreed to move to Utah and run the place.

Within days… the walk-in had food, dough was made, and employees were scheduled. And the money poured in.

Entrepreneurs build. Managers manage. And, marketers market. So, if you're dead certain you can talk your way out of a knife fight in an alley at three in the morning, fine. If you're at all uncertain, it's best to send someone who can…

So, as you move forward, be aware; yesterday's advertising media is stumbling. The Yellow Pages are dead. Print media is gasping for air. And TV is in decline. But this is not the terrifying end of marketing… just marketing as we knew it.

Reaching eager audiences has never been easier. Social media gives you access to everyone, virtually free. It also makes you more vulnerable than ever. Auto-pilot marketing programs, previously too expensive for the small guy, are now affordable, making giant companies… nervous as squirrels.

We're embarking on a voyage to a brand new world now. An experienced guide will most likely provide you the adventure and riches you're looking for. But, you can certainly go it on your own if you want to. As an entrepreneur, your success is a direct reflection of your ability to recognize the strengths and weaknesses of others, and more importantly – yourself. Bon Voyage…

Mass Advertising is Dead

Around 65 million years ago a cataclysmic event shook the entire planet. Once powerful predators died where they stood. As the dust settled, small furry creatures emerged from the safety of bushes, holes and trees… they tentatively explored their new surroundings. This mass extinction presented inquisitive, daring creatures with unrestrained opportunities. Those that quickly mastered their new environment thrived. Those late to the game are now just a part of the fossil record.

The Internet is today's earth-shattering event. The nimble entrepreneur can graze the same grass, drink from the same watering hole and travel the same paths as their fiercest competitors. In an online world, a fat TV budget is no longer the crushing advantage it used to be.

At a 1% response rate, direct mass-mail is an expensive proposition where you're often paying to reach 100 people just to find one prospect that shows any interest. That means you waste 99% of your money the minute you drop the mail at the Post Office.

Why not just pay to reach the exact people who are actively searching for what you have to offer? When they come to you, they're hot… their wallet is in their hand. You don't need to wage a "selling" battle. You simply need to make them comfortable with their decision and assure them that they can't make a mistake.

The greatest opportunity in the history of marketing has been unleashed. For the first time ever, a small start-up business with a few thousand dollars can present an image every bit as professional as a multinational corporation. In fact, what's somewhat puzzling – is that many deep-pocket, huge conglomerates have failed to recognize and embrace this shift. Many are still applying offline methods in an online world.

Up to now, maybe you haven't enjoyed the luxury of an enormous budget that can be squandered all over the place in search of traction. That means you don't have to shift gears and unlearn yesterday's habits. You have the advantage of diving head first into the future with no baggage from the past.

The same "customer focused" rules apply though. For example: Some of my Repeat Returns clients use plastic cards to operate their customer rewards program. Having had a bad experience with a plastic card manufacturer, I searched the web for a replacement. A really slick looking website got my attention. They had a bunch of whiz-bang calculators and card designing software on the site… it appeared top-notch.

And so, we began sending a few orders to this new company to try them out. Immediately we had problems, so I jumped on a plane and traveled across the country to pay a visit.

I arrived unannounced at a makeshift aluminum building resembling a tool shed. My stunned "account executive" was visibly shaken, and the owner was too embarrassed to come out of his cramped office to meet me. Their fancy website masked a pathetic fly-by-night operation. Had they performed as well as their website looked, I'd have never made the excursion. They pulled me in with their cool website, but they lost me when it came to delivering the goods.

Even on TV, you see more and more businesses advertising their website – not their product. They use their 30 seconds to induce you to visit their site. Smart. That's because a well crafted website can sell a product much better than a quick TV spot. And if you remember the "two-step" from earlier, you'll appreciate the potential.

Thirty seconds is plenty of time to create an "open loop" that drives curious prospects to a place where they can explore, and become completely engaged with a well-crafted message.

Will you rush out and switch to Geico Insurance because of a slick TV commercial? No. But you can easily visit their site to see how much money you could save. Once there… they can begin to fuel your specific desires, let you push your own hot-buttons, and serve up a tailor-made offer just for you.

65 million years ago, small creatures began displacing extinct and dying behemoths. Today, small business owners are tentatively sniffing at a new and unexplored landscape. Many large competitors with their never-ending ad budgets continue to use offline tactics – online, where they look foolish.

The Internet crashed like a meteor right smack-dab in the middle of big corporate dominance. You are right now, on the threshold of a period of unprecedented opportunity.

The scramble is on.

World of Mouth

Now Year's Eve 2009 rang in more than a fresh year. It also rang in the ascent of the "Net" generation (they're the ones wielding Blackberries). They now outnumber baby-boomers and your marketing needs to adapt – quickly.

In a recent conversation with Eric Qualman, a social media expert and author of the book "Socialnomics" Eric bombarded me with reams of undeniable statistics pointing to a once-in-a-lifetime opportunity for nimble business owners.

For example...

Radio took 38 years to arrive at 50 million listeners. TV hit that same milestone in 13 years. Shockingly, the Internet added 50 million in just 4 years... but Facebook added 100 million users in just – 9 months! If Facebook were a country – it would be the third most populated country on earth.

- 96% of 18-34-year-olds belong to some type of social network

- 1 out of 8 marriages in the U.S. last year were the result of meeting "online"

- 86% of purchases are influenced more by friends – than by advertising

Broadly speaking... If you have 1,000 customers... half of them are most likely generation "Y" and 96% of them – 480 or so – belong to a social network of some kind... most likely Facebook (upper-income), or MySpace (blue-collar).

The average Facebook member has 120 "friends." Here's where it gets interesting. 480 customers on Facebook X 120 "friends" = 57,600. Your reach is staggering.

Now, certainly – there will be a lot of overlap... many of them share the "same" friends. But still, these numbers should give you goose bumps. If only you recognize this opportunity and move quickly.

Beware: Facebook and Twitter are not venues to "advertise" on.

Social etiquette is the key. You'll kill the opportunity by using "offline" advertising. Instead, understand "why" people are on Facebook and Twitter.

Facebook

Your Facebook page should be more about you... and a little bit about your restaurant. It's "Bob" who enjoys skiing, has three kids, two dogs... and loves to cook. That's why you opened "Bob's Pizza" over on Main Street. Get it?

People love doing business with people they know. It actually makes people feel important to "know" the owner. They could really care less about the "business." They are on Facebook – to socialize with YOU.

Twitter

There are a lot of clueless restaurant owners running around tweeting out offers every other day. Wrong, wrong, wrong. People subscribe to Twitter to be kept in the loop... to know "what's going on."

And a great way to look at it is: You just arrived at a party... some people are huddled together having a conversation... you approach... listen in for a few minutes. Then you "join" the conversation. You don't just run up and start blathering about yourself.

Twitter for example... Don't tweet out "Buy one get one free." Tweet: "Fresh batch of antipasti salad... I've stashed some for you in the cooler..."

YouTube

70% of 18-to-34-year-olds watch TV on the web, and YouTube is now the second largest search engine in the world. At last year's Pizza Expo, I scanned the audience with a camcorder... and then broadcast the video to them from YouTube within 5 minutes. They marveled at the ease and rapidity of going "live" to the world.

How would you use this? Simple. There's a children's party at your pizzeria. You take a few minutes of video... and post it to YouTube. But you also embed the video on your website. Then you walk out with a laptop and show the kids. What will those kids do the minute they get home? That's right... call every single friend they know – and send them to your website.

As Eric states it: "This is the biggest shift in the human experience since the industrial revolution." The new buzzwords are Facebook, Twitter, and YouTube. There are... and will be others.

Rage Control

"In the future, everyone will be famous for 15 megabytes."

A while back, I was eyeballing a client's Facebook page when I noticed a link to Citysearch.com. I clicked, and began scanning customer reviews. Ouch! Two out of ten were a bit nasty. And, unfortunately, my client can't hit the delete key and make them go away. Maybe some are deserved, maybe not. Maybe a competitor had everyone they know – go and post some dirt. What's disturbing though is that behind the anonymity of a keyboard and an Internet connection, some people can rant as though their very survival depends on spewing rage in every direction.

Between blogs, chat rooms, and social media sites, bad news travels at light-speed, whether it is deserved – or not. In this unregulated world-wide forum, where anyone can say anything about anybody with little chance of consequences... you must meet fire with fire.

One reason my Repeat Returns program has a built-in method for collecting customer testimonials, is because it enables my clients to effortlessly build an army of raving fans. Imagine, automatically gathering dozens, or even hundreds of positive customer testimonials to post wherever, and whenever you see fit.

You really need a systematic method in place to collect written testimonials from satisfied customers. Then, when that occasional lunatic starts trashing you, you can instantly mobilize your own army and do a smack-down before any real damage occurs.

An additional benefit to collecting written testimonials from customers is because once they've gone on record; they become more locked into that position. Simply writing a positive review about you – further confirms to them, how much they really do appreciate you. This is the reason behind all those contests you've seen where you're invited to write in 100 words or less "why you love company X."

Keep an eye out for loose cannons. Do occasional Google searches on your business name to see who's saying what. And consider using Google Alerts. That way, you'll be automatically notified when your business or name pops up on the web. And certainly acknowledge and correct legitimate issues.

In the good old days, a disgruntled customer would trash you to five or six people. Today, the average person has more than 100 "friends" on Facebook, and they can get the message out on their mobile device before they leave your parking lot.

Desperation Versus Appreciation

Desperate people do desperate things… like murdering their profits in an effort to increase their profits.

What crosses your mind when you see a business relentlessly advertise items at 50% off, or buy-one-get-one-free? Any business that has to bribe you and constantly slash prices just to get you to come in, takes on the persona of a grubby beggar. The stink of desperation wafts in the air.

Now, contrast that with a business that rewards you for being a good customer. They recognize you, give you spiffs, and make you feel special and important. They continually look you in the eye, smile, and show their appreciation.

One begs. The other rewards. It's the difference between night and day. Making the shift from desperation marketing to appreciation marketing is life changing. It replaces bargain-hunters with people who *enjoy* spending money with you.

Furthermore, *bribing* conditions customers to *wait* for a discount. This begins a vicious boom and bust marketing cycle where short bursts of discount traffic fizzle into a long droughts of little traffic at all.

Rewarding on the other hand, conditions customers to *repeatedly return* and spend money with you. The more they spend with *you*, the better it gets for *them*. This builds a reliable steady flow of spending that you can count on to pay your bills and grow your business.

But don't take my word for it. Aberdeen Research Group published a study confirming what other smart business owners have already figured out. On average, companies with a solid rewards marketing program have:

- 280% higher sales
- 53% higher compound growth
- 300% higher customer retention

The success our own merchants enjoy further pours gas on this already blazing fact. Most see $100 in spending for every $2 or $3 invested in the program.

So let's get our heads straight. Bribing *prospects* to try you out is completely acceptable. Bribing *customers* just to get them to come back – is suicidal... and over time repositions you as a discount joint. Now that's fine... if that's your dream. If it's not though, slap yourself right now. Hard.

With that thought firmly rooted... come with me now to a new world where customers actually *enjoy* spending money with you and look forward to the next opportunity to do so. In fact, they almost uncontrollably insist that their friends and family do the same. This excursion takes us to a little known and lightly traveled path, a short-cut if you will... to the undiscovered treasure locked right now – inside your own business.

Customer Control

If you gave me a nickel and I gave you a dollar – would you be cool with that? You'd probably dig in your pockets and try to find more nickels – right? And if I told you – you could make that investment every day... month after month, year after year... you'd obviously be excited as a newly-minted lottery winner. Am I correct?

Well, you just saw how my Repeat Returns marketing program regularly hands back $100 for every two to three bucks invested in it. In fact we post the real live ROI on our website – updated every day for the world to see. This is real proof that marketing to your own customers is the most lucrative investment any business owner can make. But oddly enough... most small business owners couldn't get a hold of a customer right now – if their life depended on it.

All they can do is tap their fingers and wait. If the customer hasn't been lured away by a competitor or lost interest, surely – they'll eventually return. Maybe.

But why take the chance?

Ask yourself... who is more likely to visit your business today... someone who has never been there... or someone who has?

Second... mass advertising – even with steep discounts – has on average a 2% response rate – which means you waste 98% of your money the minute you write the check.

And if that wasn't bad enough... those that *do* respond – are mostly your own regular customers. They don't even need the steep discount – but they *will* use them... and this really murders your profits. In fact, your own customers (not new ones) are the highest users of discount offers. And this is the opposite of what you're shooting for.

So, reaching out to your current customers, through expensive and wasteful mass-advertising – with suicidal discounts... doesn't seem to make any sense at all... no matter how you look at it... does it?

Funny then, that most small business owners follow that strategy to the letter.

But, what if you could increase visits and spending from current customers... effortlessly, automatically, and completely hands-off – think about that for a minute. What if – you could reach them at a tiny fraction of the cost of traditional advertising? And what if – you could make your customers actually ENJOY spending more money with you – not by keeping them addicted to constant discounts... but by rewarding them for spending MORE money with you? Starting to make a little sense here, aren't we?

In fact, doesn't it make complete sense to arm yourself with an affordable, automatic way to reach out to those people most likely to buy from you – with the *frequency* required to generate additional visits and spending? You should be nodding your head up and down right now.

Now imagine you own a business and customers wander in twice a month. What if you could just **generate one extra visit** per month from them? That alone would increase your sales by 50%... and your personal income would soar because your fixed cost remains the same.

The Profit-Packed Power of "One More Visit"...

EXAMPLE: Business "X" operates on a 20% profit margin. They have 2000 customers spending $10 each time and buying 10 times each year. Look what a simple 10% improvement in customers, ticket average and total visits do to profits.

	2000 customersX $10 X 10	2200 customersX $11 X 11
Gross Sales	$200,000	$266,200
Rent	$25,000	$25,000
COGS	$50,000	$72,066
Labor	$50,000	$50,000
Other Fixed Overhead	$25,000	$25,000
Profit	$50,000	$94,134
		(88.2% increase)

Most business owners won't need to staff any more labor to handle a 10% sales increase... so the only rise is "cost of goods sold." This is where smart business owners make their money, not by constantly chasing after new customers with crazy discounts.

Sadly though, sporadic, impersonal saturation marketing complete with steep discounts remains the *only* contact most businesses ever have with even their *best* customers. They squander a fortune attracting prospects... only to completely ignore them until the next costly advertising blitz. They remain trapped in a spinning vortex of... ***Spend, Acquire, and Lose.***

This revolving door mentality opens a life-changing opportunity for you. It's the rapidly growing world of rewards marketing. We must make a significant distinction though, between obsolete programs that cost you money, and a rewards program that makes you money.

Tinker-toy programs like punch cards; and most built-in POS loyalty programs just keep handing out points like candy. Those programs are dangerous to your profits. They are *passive*, waiting for the customer to return. You shouldn't even be using them.

You want an *active* program that repeatedly reaches out to customers and gives them continual reminders and reasons to return. A program that keeps you "top of mind." Look at it this way, very simple… which business would you rather own?

- Business "A" offers points and discounts… but never communicates with their customers… (out of sight – out of mind)…

- Business "B" offers points and *rewards* too, but they also aggressively promote their business, make their customers feel appreciated and special by treating them to continual money saving offers, "insider" benefits and special perks. They stay in touch with customers, giving them frequent and compelling reasons to return and spend money – over and over and over…

Business "A" passes like a ship in the night… while business "B" is packed – every day *and* night.

And don't bamboozle yourself just because you may have low prices and/or great service. Ever heard of Southwest Airlines? They're known for rock-bottom prices and the friendliest service in the business. They stayed on the sidelines as other airlines launched frequent flyer programs. To their horror, they discovered their best customers; the business travelers – were abandoning them for other airlines that had rewards programs. A mistake they deeply regretted, but quickly fixed by launching a program in 1987. Today, their program is widely popular.

Consider this: Whether a customer buys from you once or a thousand times, your initial marketing cost is the same. The only thing that changes over time is your return on investment. Every time that customer makes a purchase, your cost to acquire that customer goes down and your profits go up.

The competitive landscape is ripe with predators. They want your customers. They need your customers. They actively hunt your customers. And if you think your safe from their voracious appetites. Think again.

Southwest Airlines is known for low prices and great service. A pretty unbeatable combination. They dallied as other airlines implemented. Slap. Even eBay has a rewards program.

A rewards program enables you to almost effortlessly accumulate a customer database... and more importantly – turn that database into a never ending river of cash.

Combination to the Safe

I've seen everyone from orthopedic surgeons to retired grandmothers pour their life savings into a small restaurant or business without a clue of how they might make it successful. I've talked with many who have just given up, as if they'd had the life squeezed out of them. Too many have poured vast oceans of cash into saturation marketing, gotten little or nothing from it... and then become galvanized in the opinion that marketing just doesn't work. They're defeated and demoralized. They are now convinced that marketing is just a waste of money. They've become helpless victims.

"Reality rookies" blame others – and everything else for their misfortunes. And as long as "someone or something else" is causing their problems – they remain powerless to solve them. Why? Because they are at the mercy of *others*. All they can do is stand by and watch help-lessly as all they've worked for goes hurtling towards disaster. After all "it's out of their hands." There's nothing they can do. And so the bull-dozer crushes them where they stand.

In contrast... others can acknowledge that – "*I* have a problem..." "*I* screwed up..." "*I* made a mistake..." which places them in control – because now *they* have the power to undo, change, and fix anything because all roads lead back to – them. Not *others*. They have the power to move. To do something.

Yes, the mere act of taking full responsibility – will force you to do one of two things: Turn your head and ignore the problem, or... deal with it. But at least now – you have two options instead of none.

Case Study: One of my clients, concerned about slumping sales secretly bought a competitor's pepperoni pizza. He told employees and customers that he was trying a new pepperoni and would like to know which one they preferred... ooops! Almost everyone picked the competitor's pizza over his. It took guts to do that – and to face the truth. But look at the power it gave him. He knows his product is infe-rior – and needs to be improved.

Sadly, many business owners come to see marketing as a necessary evil. The mere thought of spending another nickel on it – gives them conniption fits. They don't get it. It's not marketing itself that's the problem... it's *their* marketing. And it can be fixed... if only they'll admit they need help.

But, not everyone is cut out to succeed. Some are twitchy as rabbits at the thought of trying something new or different. Doing nothing shields them from the responsibility of making a mistake.

My Repeat Returns Program for example: It's proven to generate $100 in customer spending for every $2 or $3 invested. And there are no contracts. You can quit any time. Yet there is always someone who fixates on the cost. Rather than embrace a swelling ocean of automatic profit, their minds churn like a busted garbage disposal... on the *cost*.

They'll look me in the eye, and with a straight face, struggle to convince me – they can't afford $250 for the combination to a safe containing $10,000. So, when someone even starts whimpering about the cost of the program – I kindly end the conversation. If they're obsessed with chasing goldfish while Moby Dick swims away… it's just not a good fit.

It's never really how much you spend; it's what you *get* from it that matters. Good marketing is never an expense. It is the life blood of the business. The main premise of this book has been about becoming your customer and viewing your business through their eyes. Once you've crossed that threshold, your marketing pretty much creates itself.

So, where do we stand? Are you squinting through the scope… or are you in the crosshairs?

I've shared much of what I've learned about going from zero to over a million in sales. You'll find an even deeper treasure-trove of resources on my website. **www.karingtongroup.com.** It's pretty clear that putting yourself in the customer's shoes is a good start. And that with each "touch" you have with customers…

…you'll gain more by giving, than you will by taking.

When I think of marketing, I'm reminded of my flight training in the sunny skies over Stockton, California. It's overwhelming at first. New knobs, dials and pedals. So much to learn. So much to absorb.

Then, after awhile… take-offs, landings, and cross-country journeys are as familiar as a drive to the store. But flying, just like business can set you free, or get dicey in a hurry. So the training involves emergency procedures and recovery techniques. You may never need them, but then again you just might.

For example… flying at night in certain circumstances, without a visual reference point – something to signal "up and down" you can become convinced you are in straight and level flight… when you're completely *upside down*. Just like riding a roller coaster loop-de-loop while blindfolded, centrifugal force keeps your butt planted firmly in the seat. Your senses betray you. And as your altimeter plunges in this topsy-turvy environment your first impulse is to pull back on the wheel. After all, pulling back makes it go higher – right? Follow your first instincts – and you'll die. You must do the *opposite*.

Regrettably… going into business doesn't require any preparation at all. No manuals, No emergency training. Anyone can do it. And of course the failure rate is spectacular. And no wonder so many push the discount button at the first sign of trouble. It "feels" like the right move to make at the time.

And the spiral begins.

What seems like it should take you *up*… actually takes you *down*. It just doesn't make any sense. And what's really perplexing… is that so many come to believe, doing more and more of what's clearly not working, will somehow work – *this* time. Digging faster and faster, and harder and harder… only makes the hole deeper, faster.

It's best not to overthink it.

What will you do now?

Will you build the amazing life you've dreamed of? Will your children go to college? Will you travel to exotic destinations? Will you provide security and stability for loved ones? Will you be able to ask yourself that terrible question?

"If someone held a gun to my head and told me I needed to get one brand new customer to buy my product at full price within 24 hours or they would pull the trigger… what would I do?"

Will it focus your mind like it did mine? After all… doesn't your life depend on that answer?

Death Spiral

Vancouver Tower – Cessna 2753 Lima… declaring an emergency…

Dusk, 1986, I pull back on the wheel of my four-seat Cessna 172. Myself, Nancy and two friends have flown up from Tacoma, Washington to enjoy a nice dinner in Canada. We climb smoothly into the night skies above Vancouver International Airport. The weather report promises "clear skies." It is however, getting *very* dark. As we climb past 1200 feet I notice a temporary blackout. Vancouver's glow, now to my left, blinks out. I can't see anything. Then I glimpse ships and far off city lights. Then black. Then clear. Then finally, the last remaining fragments of luminosity are squeezed from the sky… replaced by a vice of darkness. Pitch black darkness.

Spinning three feet away, just beyond the edges of my vision, the propeller can only be heard now. The moisture-rich atmosphere has condensed into a thick blanket of fog. Man it was fast. I fly along another minute or two waiting for it to break. It doesn't. The world outside our bubble has been extinguished. I'm in trouble. *We're* in trouble. Grave trouble. I am *not* instrument rated – and I am flying blind – over the ocean. Great…

Without a moments hesitation, I grab my mic and call "Vancouver tower – Cessna 2753 Lima flying IFR – I am not instrument rated." At the same time I'm talking – I twist the dials on my navigation radio to 7700 and push the green button. I've just declared an emergency. My aircraft lights up like a Christmas tree on their radar screen. They know exactly where I am. Funny thing though, they may not need to assist me after all because…

I'm already fully engulfed in a death spiral…

Yep. After punching in the emergency code – I glance down at my instruments. Left wing *low*, descending *rapidly* through 800 feet. My eyelids rise. Mortified, my mind performs a quick calculation. We've plunged 400 feet in *less* than 30 seconds. The clock on the dash ticks off two seconds. My heart slams in my chest. Adrenaline pours into my mind. Impact in less than half a minute. Pull back… pull back… NO!

What?! What?! Remember... Moving too quickly now... 600 feet... Think! Think! 500 feet... Death is coming for us. Ready to strike. I can smell it.

Time freezes.

Little girls take great pleasure in cutting out paper dolls, baking cookies, giggling and just being silly. Thankfully, my daughters are safe at grandma's house tonight. A mosaic of happy memories brings a brief smile. A smile that is quickly replaced by an emptiness as vast and untouchable as deep interstellar space. I will never see them again.

Years ago my mother gave me a simple gift. It didn't cost anything, yet it remains priceless. In her darkest moment, with her life draining away, she whispered: "Kamron, I love you."

And now, sadly, surrounded by darkness, and with time running out I had no hugs to hug. No kisses to kiss. No gifts to give. Tick...

No! Dammit! Not tonight...

A voice echoes in the blackness...

Suddenly, I'm in the warm, sunny skies over Stockton California. The fields are spinach green. The sky brilliant blue, like the base of a gas flame. My flight instructor, Robert Jensen is seated next to me. We're in a gut wrenching spiral. He's barking out orders. Yes!... I've trained for *this!*

Blue skies vanish. Calm replaces fear. Darkness returns. Time is short. A difficult decision is made. I must *maintain* the dive... in fact, actually push the wheel into it... an unsettling thought.

"Vancouver tower calling Cessna 2753 Lima – over."

The initial burst of acceleration is petrifying. An unforgiving ocean rushes up in the blackness.

"53 Lima – 53 Lima – state your altitude – over."

I press right rudder and gently apply right wheel. Descending... 350 feet... the clock ticks... 300 feet... tick... wings level... tick... pull back... tick. The instruments confirm straight and level flight... tick... *pull up!*

"Vancouver tower, Cessna 2753 lima straight and level at 300, beginning to climb – over…"

"Cessna 2753 Lima – Whidbey Island Naval Air Station – we'll take it from here… over"

Forty heart-stopping minutes after declaring an aviation emergency, the fog releases us to a carnival of twinkling lights rising up from Seattle. We pass safely on our journey. I've never felt more alive. It's surprising the amazing wealth of resources you can access… when your life and everything most precious to you… is on the line.

I've been blessed with opportunity, second chances, amazing luck and intense personal success. My hope is that you've discovered in these pages, something, *anything* that will help illuminate a brighter, more certain path that takes you where you desire. And that when you need it most, when your life depends on it…

…that Fate will reach out and extend his hand to you, as he has so many times to me…

Epilogue

As I gaze back across the years… I can only wonder at how a weird, dark question illuminated a new and amazing journey. And how stunningly fast it cut through all the crap, giving me a moment of crystal clear clarity. "What if?"

Seems like sometimes you just need to get rattled. Well, why not just rattle yourself before a competitor beats you to it? Indeed, the sooner the better, before you wake up one day and wonder what just happened to your youth, your dreams, your vitality…

Interviews with the survivors of catastrophes show an interesting pattern. Survivors begin moving quickly at the very first sign of trouble. Their minds racing towards solutions, not hunting for obstacles. Almost any action is better than staying where trouble is.

And just like in a Hollywood movie, there's always some idiot frozen by a flash of fear and panic… who snaps and starts yelling "We're all gonna DIE!"… Until the hero smacks him upside the head.

Across the landscape today, in every city and town, once stable businesses will begin to slip. Deep-pocket competitors will open shop. And the local buffoon will lower prices, yet again. And most business owners, as though helpless bystanders to an unfolding tragedy – will panic. And panic fosters poor decisions. The shocking failure rate bears this out.

But heroes will emerge. Those who zig, when the crowd zags. Those who always manage to wriggle free from the clutches of failure. One of *them*, might as well be *you*.

Utahn Wounds Ex-Wife, Kills Self After Fight

Special to The Tribune

HOLLADAY — A 35-year-old man shot and killed himself Friday afternoon following a fight with his ex-wife, during which she was critically wounded.

Sheriff's Detective Samuel W. Dawson said Don E. Stewart, no address available, went to the home of his former wife, Shirley Stewart, 35, 4426-2990 East, held her and three children at gunpoint, then forced Mrs. Stewart to drive him and two of the children through the surrounding area.

Sheriff's Deputy James C. Luff said Mrs. Stewart was driving northbound on I-215 at about 4200 South when Mr. Stewart apparently told her to slow down. When she complied, the pistol went off. She was struck in the right side and, according to lawmen, Mr. Stewart shot himself in the head when he realized what had happened. He died at 5:15 p.m. at St. Mark's Hospital. Mrs. Stewart was listed in critical condition late Friday at the same hospital.

Detective Dawson said the sheriff's office was notified of the incident before the shooting occurred and patrol cars were in the area looking for the vehicle.

Deputy Luff said sheriff's cars arrived almost immediately after the shooting, followed by Salt Lake County paramedic crews, who quickly administered medical care to the injured woman.

August 17, 1974
Salt Lake Tribune

Afterword

My mother survived her injuries. And every August 16th since that day… I've called my mother or taken her out to lunch.

I handed this off to a few friends to look over before it hit the presses… several told me, they felt just a bit more information or detail to close the twenty year gap between August of 74 and November of 94 would satisfy a bit of curiosity. And to be sure… many were blindsided by the events of August, 1974. I've rarely brought it up. One friend made the statement; "That must have scarred you for life."

It did not.

Other than the occasional dreams… that episode never crosses my mind.

Some also wondered why I didn't share more of my personal stories… which I'll admit – some are pretty wild.

The answer to that? This book is about you – not me.

So, rather than add to these pages… if you're interested you'll find a bit of history along with some photos at my website:

www.karingtongroup.com.

And, if you ever want to know about the hacksaw blade I found in a jail cell… why I woke up one morning in a cow pasture… how I managed to sell a warehouse that didn't belong to me… why Hells Angels once took me to the hospital… what prompted a cop to arrest me –

then abruptly release me and speed away... how spending my last twenty bucks led to my first major financial success... why a customer at a restaurant I worked at filed charges because he was beaten up in the parking lot for not ordering dessert... or even how I ended up in juvenile hall for the first time at the age of – eight... just ask me. We'll have some fun.

KK

Kamron Karington's background is unique – to say the least. His first stint in Juvenile Hall was at the age of eight. His report cards were littered with Ds and Fs. And he dropped out of school in ninth grade. Then, he started selling real estate at 18, became a Dee-jay at 20, was flying his own airplane at the age of 23, o p e n e d the first of four nightclubs at 26, produced a hit record at 30, and then… one night, while making a phone call to g e t tickets to the Rolling Stones – Kamron ended up buying a run-down pizza restaurant. (Huh?) Massive frustration and an impending sense of defeat just about sunk the venture until an odd night spent on top of a walk-in cooler led to an immediate and stunning turn of fate. The struggling business catapulted from $3,000 a week to $1.6 million a year. All told, a remarkable 1,066% increase.

In 2003, Kamron released the *"Black Book"* – a 450 page marketing course, the blueprint behind his massive success (it sold out worldwide at $597 a copy). The Black Book became one of the top-selling marketing courses of its kind in the world. And now, *Gun to the Head Marketing* distills a lifetime of real world "hands on" sales building experience into one thought provoking (and some say "controversial") concept that cuts through the marketing haze like a hot knife through butter. As a result, Kamron is an "in demand" speaker. His live training events and seminars are wildly popular and widely attended. He's taught thousands of business owners around the world how to explode past limiting frustrations, take iron-grip control of their marketing, and generate predictable streams of newfound profits.